GOD'S PLANS
FOR YOUR
FINANCES

DWIGHT NICHOLS

 *Whitaker House*

GOD'S PLANS FOR YOUR FINANCES

Dwight Nichols
Urban Impact Ministries
P.O. Box 901
North Little Rock, AR 72115
Phone (501) 372-1455

ISBN: 0-88368-509-4
Printed in the United States of America
Copyright © 1998 by Whitaker House

Whitaker House
30 Hunt Valley Circle
New Kensington, PA 15068

Nichols, Dwight, 1948–
    God's plans for your finances / by Dwight Nichols.
        p.   cm.
    ISBN 0-88368-509-4 (trade paper)
    1. Finance, Personal—Religious aspects—Christianity. I. Title.
HG179.N527   1998
332.024—dc21   97-50101

3 4 5 6 7 8 9 10 11 12 13 14 15 16 / 10 09 08 07 06 05 04 03 02 01 00

CONTENTS

DEDICATION

This book is dedicated to my wife, Cynthia, and my mother and father, Josephine and Conrad Nichols. Without their love, support, and guidance over the years, I would never have made it to this point in my life.

I would also like to dedicate this book to my children, Trina, Dewayne, and Christina, in whom I am well pleased. My prayer for them is that the wisdom of God outlined in these pages will continue to serve as a guide for their lives, and that they will pass these principles on to their families so that their lives will be a living testimony of the goodness of God's provision for generations to come.

ACKNOWLEDGMENTS

I would like to take the time to express my appreciation and thanks to Janice Drennan, who went above and beyond the call of duty in assisting in every aspect of organizing this book. She made a substantial contribution of her time and resources for the completion of this project.

Special appreciation also goes to Pastor Happy Caldwell, Remo Jacuzzi, Pastor Silas Johnson, and my brothers, Richard and Larry Nichols, for their encouragement, inspiration, and contribution of time and resources. I further appreciate Debbie Warrington, who not only provided the dictating and typing skills to initiate this project, but who also has assisted me in many other projects over the past twelve years.

Last, but not least, I would like to extend special appreciation to my business partner, Don Chastek, who has provided support and encouragement for this and many other projects. His practical wisdom and realistic feedback have been stabilizing factors in my life.

FOREWORD

God has a financial system. The Bible is very clear that God gives us power (ability) to get wealth so that He can establish His covenant in the earth through us. This basic economic principle, which is clearly explained in *God's Plans for Your Finances,* is the foundation for godly prosperity. If it is overlooked, it can cause frustration, wrong motives, and abuse. Unless we understand and are grounded in the purpose for prosperity, we can become motivated by greed, personal gain, and self-preservation.

However, I have seen many believers become disillusioned or complacent after being motivated to give to the work of the Gospel but not seeing their own financial dreams realized. It is not that the Word doesn't work or that God doesn't want them to prosper. It is simply that they have no knowledge of the basic principles of biblical economics. Even if they did have prosperity, it would be short-lived.

Economics is stewardship. It is the science of how people make commonsense decisions regarding money: managing, investing, and creating wealth. An economy, by definition, is the management of the resources of a household, business, city, or government. There is no better type of economy than capitalism or free enterprise. Socialism, which our government is pushing us toward today, is the midway mark between capitalism and communism.

Communism is based on the belief that the universe is only matter and energy and nothing else. This is materialism. If man is just a product of his environment, there is no God; by giving him what he needs (food, clothing, and shelter), you can change human nature. False! Communism breeds secular humanism and totalitarianism. We know communism doesn't work. The

Bible does not teach socialism, either, but suggests free enterprise, where each individual has the right and responsibility to produce, save, invest, and create wealth.

The Scriptures teach that man and universe are both created by God and, therefore, are both spiritual and material. Man was created in God's image and given dominion over creation. Government and laws are vehicles by which God can offer protection to the innocent and punish the guilty. God is the one who taught man the basic principles of economics so that man can be a good steward over the wealth that God gave him the power and ability to produce.

There have been other books written about money management and finances. However, Dwight Nichols' approach is delightfully fresh and honest. Dwight has no hidden agendas. His motive is clear, and his purpose is to disciple the body of Christ in the use of biblical financial principles.

My favorite chapter is chapter 6 on honesty and integrity. I have never seen this area covered in money management, but it is the foundation of all God's blessings.

The principles in *God's Plans for Your Finances,* if applied in faith, will change your life.

Happy Caldwell
Pastor, Agape Church
Little Rock, Arkansas

INTRODUCTION

Repairing Broken Dreams

I was born in rural Alabama, the oldest of ten children of Conrad, Sr., and Josephine Nichols. I grew up in Prichard, Alabama, the poorest city in the state and, according to statistics from the United States Department of Health and Human Services, one of the poorest cities in the nation. Without ever realizing it, I was being programmed to have certain attitudes and expectations that would keep me bound to a specific lifestyle.

As a youngster, I had dreams of growing up to be a successful businessman, able to help my family and to reach out and help others. After years of running a small family business, these dreams became more and more distant. I began to accept the thought that maybe I had been born into the wrong race and economic background. My family did not have any money, so I did not feel that I had the corresponding privileges. I did not know anyone in my family who had been successful in business; why should I expect any more?

I began to believe that the reason I wasn't doing as well as I should was that someone else was keeping me down. It wasn't my fault. It was the government's fault, or maybe it was the fault of the environment in which I was raised.

Even though I had a college degree, I could not see myself expanding my business activities beyond the neighborhood where I grew up. I was so busy trying to make money for my family and myself that I didn't have time for anyone else. Although I was still a young man, I was trapped behind an invisible wall. I was bound by the circumstances of life and controlled by limited thinking. Although the answers actually were there all the time, I was blind to their existence.

In 1978, I started attending a Bible study session on personal finances. As a businessman, I had never recognized the Bible as a credible source of financial direction. I had been taught that it was irreverent to talk about money in church and that God is only interested in spiritual things. Nevertheless, what I learned had such an impact on me that I started an exhaustive study on my own. What I found changed the course of my life!

I began to realize that God has a financial system already in place and that the Bible outlines the plan for operating in His system. The Scriptures have much to say about how to properly use money. In fact, sixteen of the thirty-eight parables that Jesus gave in the New Testament are concerned with how to handle money and possessions.

As I continued to search the Scriptures, it was as if a veil were being lifted from my eyes. I saw that God didn't have a problem with Christians having money. Moreover, I came to understand that God's financial plan for our lives is well above the expectations of the average Christian. I had been held captive by my own attitudes and expectations. I had been locked into a certain lifestyle because I had been programmed to think in a certain way. Now I could see beyond the walls that had me locked in. As I continued to study the Scriptures, it occurred to me that it was possible to do what God's Word said I could do, and that I could have what God said I could have in regard to finances. The principles that were coming into focus before my eyes were so basic that I could not understand why I had never seen them on my own.

I began to see the mistakes I had made and the steps that should be taken to correct them. Because I took the time to learn the fundamental principles of how God's financial system works, God began to bless my finances. As a result of applying these principles, I was able to break free from the mindset that had held me captive. Although it took diligence and hard work, I was able to break the spirit of poverty over my life and get my finances under control.

Since then, my life has been an adventure. However, this is not the end of the story. Just as I thought everything was going well, I began to realize that something else was missing! In 1989, God began to stir something inside me. Although I had thought I was doing fine, God showed me that I was falling far short of His mark. He began to direct my attention to all of the economic decay around me. I saw the broken lives and broken dreams of so many people. They were caught in the clutches of poverty, with no way out. I saw people with God-given potential being swept away by a tidal wave of economic circumstances that were beyond their control. I began to empathize with the hopelessness and despair that I saw reflected in the eyes of others. My heart began to burst with compassion. I thought back to only a few short years earlier, when I had been trapped by the same spirit that is causing all the economic devastation in our urban areas.

As God brought these things to my consciousness, I realized how little things had really changed within my life. I had moved from one trap to another. Instead of running just to make a living for my family, now I was running to keep the trappings of success without considering what was happening in the lives of others around me. I struggled with God on this issue. "What can I do that would have any type of impact on all this devastation? I am only one person. It is hard enough just taking care of my own circumstances," I argued with myself and God.

"Father, I realize that these principles changed my life, but I don't have the time," I continued. "There are only so many hours in the day." I reminded God that it had taken years of trial and error for me to move from where I was financially in the past to where I was at that point. I told God that people are interested in quick fixes, not long-term solutions. Although the principles are simple and straightforward, most people are not willing to make the commitment or take the time and effort to learn the principles of financial success and then have the discipline to apply them to their lives.

God reminded me that this decision was not mine to make. Every individual would have to make the decision for himself or herself. What God wanted me to do was to be obedient and to share how these principles had changed the financial circumstances in my life. God told me to tell as many people as I could that the same principles that had transformed my life would transform their lives if they were willing to learn them and apply them to their circumstances, no matter what their race or economic background. God said, "If you are willing to take a step of faith and write down these principles as I have revealed them to you, I will do the rest."

In 1990, I decided to take two years off from the investment banking business to organize these principles into book form. God has been faithful to His Word. Churches across the country have shown an interest in using this material to teach the principles of biblical stewardship to their congregations. More importantly, I see more and more pastors beginning to make the connection between being a good steward over economic matters and being a good steward over spiritual matters. They are starting to realize that by teaching individuals to break the spirit of poverty and to impact their economic circumstances, the church is indirectly affecting the economic condition of the communities it serves.

Moreover, with my spiritual eyes, I see even more churches beginning to get serious about teaching their members the fundamentals of how to live successful lives and how to be good stewards and efficient money managers. As churches accept this aspect of their responsibility, I see people breaking free from the spirit of poverty and being able to come off welfare. I see those not directly caught in the downward economic spiral of our urban centers also becoming more effective managers of their resources. I picture them getting their finances in order so they can be in a position to reach out and extend a helping hand to others.

My prayer for you is that as you read this book, God will give you a revelation of His financial system and a revelation of the steps you can take to get your financial house in order. And, just as important to the body of Christ, as you begin to get your finances under control, my prayer is that you will reach out to at least two other families. The best way to share these principles is by letting people see them in operation in your life.

Introduction

DISCOVERING GOD'S FINANCIAL SYSTEM

God's Plans for Your Finances will help you identify the principles that govern God's financial system. The main purpose of this book is to clearly delineate the fundamentals you need in order to become a skillful manager of God's resources and to create and build wealth in God's economy.

Chapters 1–5 lay the foundation by examining God's attitude toward money and possessions and discussing what it means to be a good steward. These chapters identify the fundamental reasons why the average family is struggling with the issue of finances. They also reveal the principles that must be followed in order to build a solid foundation to receive God's financial blessing.

Chapters 6–10 provide you with principles that will help you multiply the amount of money you have to manage as a steward. They outline these principles and delineate things you can do that will bring supernatural increase. In Deuteronomy 28, the Bible teaches that the blessings of God will overtake the individual who obeys these laws as they relate to money.

Chapter 11 deals with the kind of faith you need in order to receive God's supernatural increase. Chapter 12 is the most practical of all. It outlines a twenty-one-step action plan to jump-start your personal finances. "Twenty-One Steps to Building Wealth" gives specific strategies that are necessary in order to get your financial house in order, providing you with a step-by-step plan of financial freedom guidelines that every individual should implement to build a solid financial foundation.

God wants to take the struggle out of your personal finances. By learning these principles and applying them to your everyday life, you will be prepared to receive God's supernatural increase. No matter what happens in the world economy, no matter what your current financial condition is, you will be standing on solid ground.

As I wrote earlier, I have a desire to see the local church become a strong economic force within the community that it serves. The principles outlined in God's Word can break the spirit of poverty and change the entire economic direction of a community. As each church teaches its members the basic principles of biblical economics and trains individuals within the church to teach these principles to others, it can begin to have a significant impact on the lives of its individual members. Only as we get our finances in order can we extend a helping hand to those around us.

If all of us who understand God's economic system will do our part to apply it to our lives and then reach out to share these principles with others, together we could be effective in serving the body of Christ. We could be God's instruments for repairing broken dreams. I pray that each individual who reads this book will make a firm commitment to walk in financial integrity and have a greater impact for God.

CHAPTER 1

YOUR ECONOMIC DESTINY

*But thou shalt remember the LORD thy God: for it is he that
giveth thee power to get wealth, that he may establish his
covenant which he sware unto thy fathers, as it is this day.*
—Deuteronomy 8:18

*I have been young, and now am old; yet have I not seen the
righteous forsaken, nor his seed begging bread.*
—Psalm 37:25

I was talking with Jan, a twenty-seven-year-old single parent
with two children and a full-time job. She said she could not
live on her present salary. "Well, what have you done to
change your financial circumstances? Have you asked God to
give you a creative idea?" I inquired.

She said that she had been praying about the situation for a
number of years, but there had been no change in her circumstances. She was waiting for God to intervene on her behalf.

"Do you have any kind of plan to budget your spending? Do
you set aside any portion of your current income for savings?" I
continued.

"I don't earn enough money to worry about a budget—
much less, any kind of savings," she answered.

Jan is a committed Christian and genuinely loves the Lord.
Nevertheless, she is trapped by the system and cannot see a way
out. She even has a desire to give a portion of her income to the
church, but she never seems to have enough left over after
paying her bills. She wants her circumstances to change but has
not taken any specific action that would better her financial
condition. Additionally, she has not properly managed what she

already has. She has fallen into the same economic mindset as many Christians. Jan believes that if God wanted her to have more money, He would change her financial circumstances. However, if she continues on her current path, she will never be free from the bondage of her financial situation. She will never achieve her full economic potential.

Jan is halting progress toward her economic destiny without ever realizing it! What has she done to get in this position? Is there anything she can do to change her financial circumstances? What do she and other Christians need to know about their economic potential in God?

GOD'S PLANS FOR YOUR LIFE

According to Deuteronomy 8:18, God has given each Christian the power to get wealth so that He might establish His covenant in the earth. This is part of our economic destiny. God has placed within every individual the ability to take control of personal financial circumstances, to live successful lives, and to make a positive contribution to society. Jesus has already paid the price for our prosperity, spiritually and otherwise. *"He became poor, so that you through his poverty might become rich"* (2 Corinthians 8:9). However, by the time most people become young adults, they have been programmed by a system that will keep them from reaching their full economic potential. Many will be completely controlled by the spirit of poverty. Their minds will have been programmed in such a way that they will be kept in financial bondage for the rest of their lives.

God wants to raise up individuals within the body of Christ who can be trusted with money. He wants us to get our financial houses in order, not only to meet our needs, but also so that we will be able to reach out to those around us. He wants us to be in a position to give so that His covenant might be established on earth. This will never happen in our lives unless we learn how to become good stewards over the money and resources that have already been entrusted to our care.

The years ahead will see many turbulent economic changes. Although many will be swept away by economic calamity, those who understand the principles that govern God's economic system and are found faithful in applying these principles to their lives will flourish in the midst of chaos. They will have the financial resources to meet this challenge. This is especially important, since, during these difficult times, the church will witness the greatest opportunity in its history for the harvesting of souls for the kingdom of God.

According to studies, as much as two-thirds of our population will have to depend on the government to live after retirement. A record number of individuals are already on welfare or some form of government assistance. Moreover, an even greater number of families are struggling to survive from paycheck to paycheck. Bad credit and personal bankruptcies have become commonplace. What is even more disturbing, our urban areas are deteriorating at an alarming rate. The spirit of poverty has been allowed to imprison our inner cities with an attitude that stifles creativity and discourages economic progress on an individual basis.

As disappointing as it may seem, evidence suggests that there is not much difference between the Christian and the non-Christian in regard to personal finances. The American advertising industry, often referred to as Madison Avenue, influences us to buy things we don't need; as a result, many Christians find themselves caught in the same financial bondage as the rest of the world. God cannot trust these Christians with larger amounts of money because they are not faithful with what they already have.

To those Christians who are willing to pay the price to learn how to handle money according to His guidelines, God will give supernatural abilities to receive worldly wealth. Yes, God is interested in our financial well-being. He wants to restore our families and rebuild our communities, but this can only be done on an individual-by-individual basis. We cannot depend on the government to do it. The family is the main economic unit of our society, and each family must learn how to assume the role that God originally intended for it. As Christians, we must be willing to accept our responsibility as stewards if we are going to walk in God's supernatural provision.

ATTITUDES ABOUT MONEY AND WEALTH

Your attitudes about money and wealth will determine whether you will receive the financial inheritance that is rightfully yours. What you believe governs your perspective, your thinking, and your actions as they relate to financial matters. Your actions reflect your core belief system. Therefore, it is critical that Christians realize that God has a financial system and that His system is governed by well-defined principles.

The first and most important principle governing God's financial system is a proper understanding of God's perspective on Christians having money and wealth. The following Scriptures tell us something about the way God looks at our finances:

But thou shalt remember the LORD thy God: for it is he that giveth thee power to get wealth, that he may establish his covenant which he sware unto thy fathers, as it is this day. (Deuteronomy 8:18)

Beloved, I wish above all things that thou mayest prosper and be in health, even as thy soul prospereth. (3 John 2)

The wealth of the sinner is laid up for the just. (Proverbs 13:22)

The blessing of the LORD, it maketh rich, and he addeth no sorrow with it. (Proverbs 10:22)

Let the LORD be magnified, which hath pleasure in the prosperity of his servant. (Psalm 35:27)

God does not have a problem with Christians having money as long as money does not control them. In fact, having money to carry out His purposes is part of our economic destiny. If the above Scriptures are true, then why aren't we, as Christians, walking in God's provision? Doesn't the Bible suggest that we are supposed to receive certain financial blessings if we are committed Christians or give to God's work? Why is it that so many Christians who sincerely love the Lord are struggling to survive from paycheck to paycheck?

There are major misconceptions about finances circulating in the church today that are leading Christians to believe that God can take care of all of our financial problems with the wave of His hand, without regard to the guidelines He has already given in His Word. Misconceptions about God's economic system are preventing many Christians from receiving His supernatural blessing in their lives.

Satan has been able to deceive many Christians into having the wrong attitude about money. They think that money is evil and that Christians are not supposed to have anything to do with it. This, of course, is a paradox in itself, because it takes money to live. Nevertheless, many Christians have been led to believe that there is something inherently spiritual about being poor. Some even feel that there is something wrong with being financially successful. Others feel that they don't have any control over their financial circumstances, so why should they bother themselves with such matters? This is not what the Bible teaches. The truth of the matter is that God has provided an economic legacy for His children, but we must do our part to inherit what is rightfully ours.

GOD'S SUPERNATURAL PROVISIONS

The parameters of our economic inheritance have already been determined. We are to be blessed so that we can be a blessing. Deuteronomy 28 states that if we listen diligently to the voice of the Lord and obey His principles, the blessings of God will come upon us, and overtake us. The blessings will come when we are obedient and follow God's instructions:

And it shall come to pass, if thou shalt hearken diligently unto the voice of the LORD thy God, to observe and to do all his commandments which I command thee this day, that the LORD thy God will set thee on high above all nations of the earth: and all these blessings shall come on thee, and overtake thee, if thou shalt hearken unto the voice of the LORD thy God. Blessed shalt thou be in the city, and

blessed shalt thou be in the field. Blessed shall be the fruit of thy body, and the fruit of thy ground, and the fruit of thy cattle, the increase of thy kine, and the flocks of thy sheep. Blessed shall be thy basket and thy store. Blessed shalt thou be when thou comest in, and blessed shalt thou be when thou goest out. The LORD shall cause thine enemies that rise up against thee to be smitten before thy face: they shall come out against thee one way, and flee before thee seven ways. The LORD shall command the blessing upon thee in thy storehouses, and in all that thou settest thine hand unto; and he shall bless thee in the land which the LORD thy God giveth thee. The LORD shall establish thee an holy people unto himself, as he hath sworn unto thee, if thou shalt keep the commandments of the LORD thy God, and walk in his ways. And all people of the earth shall see that thou art called by the name of the LORD; and they shall be afraid of thee. And the LORD shall make thee plenteous in goods, in the fruit of thy body, and in the fruit of thy cattle, and in the fruit of thy ground, in the land which the LORD sware unto thy fathers to give thee. The LORD shall open unto thee his good treasure, the heaven to give the rain unto thy land in his season, and to bless all the work of thine hand: and thou shalt lend unto many nations, and thou shalt not borrow. And the LORD shall make thee the head, and not the tail; and thou shalt be above only, and thou shalt not be beneath; if that thou hearken unto the commandments of the LORD thy God, which I command thee this day, to observe and to do them.
(Deuteronomy 28:1–13)

Our economic heritage is much broader than just paying bills and meeting our needs. It is not just money. It is an attitude that causes us to understand the true purpose and use of money: to establish a sound financial base for our families and also be able to reach out and extend a helping hand to others. This economic inheritance has already been established; the legal parameters have been set, and the conditions have been outlined in His Word. The rest is up to us!

WHY ARE THE RICH GETTING RICHER
AND THE POOR GETTING POORER?

Through Christ, believers have been given victory over poverty and lack:

> *The Spirit of the Lord is upon me, because he hath anointed me to preach the gospel to the poor; he hath sent me to heal the brokenhearted, to preach deliverance to the captives, and recovering of sight to the blind, to set at liberty them that are bruised.* (Luke 4:18)

> *But my God shall supply all your need according to his riches in glory by Christ Jesus.* (Philippians 4:19)

Yet, many Christians' lives are being destroyed because of the spirit of poverty. It is important for us to realize that we have a role to play in applying God's financial plan to our lives. We must become knowledgeable about the laws of increase and multiplication that are outlined in the Scriptures.

During the time when I was working in the investment banking and securities industry, I dealt with both wealthy individuals and institutional accounts, and I made a very important discovery. Some people make money regardless of the condition of the economy or whether the market goes up or down. It seemed unfair to me that the people who had the most money appeared to be getting more money, while the people who needed money were doing without. So I asked God this question: "Why are the rich getting richer and the poor getting poorer?"

One day, while I was studying the Bible and meditating on His Word, God began to reveal the answer. He has put certain principles into operation on earth regarding money, and they will work for whomever uses them. When it rains, it rains on the just and the unjust alike (Matthew 5:45).

The better you manage your money, the more money comes your way. Conversely, if you don't manage your money properly, the funds that you do have will never be enough. They will be taken away from you. This principle is documented throughout the Bible, but perhaps the most graphic illustration of it is in the following passage of Scripture:

Take therefore the talent [money] *from him, and give it unto him which hath ten talents. For unto every one that hath shall be given, and he shall have abundance: but from him that hath not shall be taken away even that which he hath. And cast ye the unprofitable servant into outer darkness.*   (Matthew 25:28–30)

Notice that the money was taken away from the one who had the least and given to the one who had the most—the one who got the best results from what had already been entrusted to his care. The one who demonstrated through past actions that he knew how to get the best return was given that which was taken away from the one who had the least. It is what we do with what we have that gets God's attention!

The rich are getting richer because they understand the fundamental principles that govern the building of wealth, and they manage these principles in their favor. On the other hand, the poor are getting poorer because they do not understand how to properly manage the resources they have.

Like Jan, many Christians are trapped in economic bondage because of wrong attitudes. They are waiting for God to perform a miracle to turn their finances around when the means are already within their reach. In fact, God has already made provisions regarding our financial circumstances. But, because we think we don't have any control over our financial destiny, we don't properly take advantage of the provisions God has already made available for us. We have, in essence, locked God out of working in our financial circumstances.

MYTHS AND RELIGIOUS TRADITIONS

Our money is important to God; it can be a powerful tool in the hands of faithful Christians. Because of the impact that this truth can have for the kingdom of God and the powerful blow it can deliver to the kingdom of darkness, Satan has gone to great lengths to keep the church confused regarding the role of money in the life of a believer.

Through myths and religious traditions, Satan has been very successful in keeping us confused regarding our economic destiny. We have been programmed to have the wrong attitudes about money. Satan has provided a steady flow of partial truths mixed with distortions to keep us confused in the area of proper money management.

These myths and religious traditions surface in many forms. Often, they vary according to one's cultural and economic background. See if you can recognize any of these fables:

1. "Money is the root of all evil." It is corrupt and leads people astray. Therefore, you should not be concerned with money and material possessions. If a person has money, he or she must be stealing from someone.

2. "I'm as poor as old Job's turkey (hen)." Poverty is a sign of spirituality. God took away all of Job's material possessions; therefore, it is wrong for us to try to build wealth while we are here on earth. True Christians should live a life of poverty in order to demonstrate their genuine love for God.

3. "Jesus had nowhere to lay his head" (Matthew 8:20). Jesus was poor and had no worldly possessions; therefore, as followers of Jesus, we should be poor as well.

4. "It is easier for a camel to go through the eye of a needle than it is for a rich person to go to heaven" (Matthew 19:24); therefore, you can't have worldly wealth on earth and expect to go to heaven, too.

5. Jesus told a rich young ruler to sell his possessions and give his money away (Luke 18:18–22); therefore, if you love Jesus and want to serve God, you should take a vow of poverty. You will obtain your riches when you get to heaven.

6. "All preachers want to do is to get your money," or, "Money is part of the world's economic system, and Christians are supposed to be heavenly minded; therefore, the church

should only function as a place to worship God, and it should stay out of people's business and personal affairs."

7. God answers prayer; therefore, if you really trust in Jesus and exert faith, He will meet all your financial needs. You don't have to do anything about your circumstances. Just pray, and take one day at a time.

8. You should be content with what you have (Hebrews 13:5); therefore, you don't have to plan ahead. God will take care of your circumstances. If you were born on the wrong side of the tracks, there is nothing that you can do about it. You should be content with where you are.

9. Jesus was interested only in spiritual things, not material possessions; therefore, it is wrong to talk about money in church. Church is not the place for that kind of thing.

10. You should not charge your brother interest (Deuteronomy 23:19); therefore, you should not have savings and investment accounts that pay interest.

11. You are not supposed to lay up treasures for yourself on earth (Matthew 6:19) or hoard up money; therefore, you should not have surplus or savings accounts. Having bank accounts limits your trust in God.

12. When a person tithes (gives ten percent of his or her income to God's work) or gives extra offerings to further the cause of the Gospel, God is automatically bound to meet all of that person's financial requirements, even if he or she doesn't follow the other principles that govern money, which are outlined in the Bible.

At the core of every myth is a distorted biblical principle. Many of our attitudes about God's provisions are distorted because of misinformation. On the surface, these fables may sound humorous or even very religious. Yet, even though none of the above concepts are true, they grip the hearts and souls of Christians and non-Christians alike. These traditions have been responsible for robbing us of our economic inheritance. As a result of these misrepresentations, many Christians don't feel comfortable even talking about money in church.

One of the primary purposes of *God's Plans for Your Finances* is to dispel these myths by shining the light of God's Word on them. God has outlined principles in the Bible that would allow us to avoid the typical scenario that holds the average family hostage, if we would just follow them. We can take the struggle out of our finances. By applying the basic fundamentals of biblical stewardship to their own personal finances, Christians can overcome the obstacles that are keeping them in financial bondage.

LACK OF KNOWLEDGE

Another reason why many Christians are having difficulties with their personal finances is that they lack knowledge about the Word of God: *"My people are destroyed for lack of knowledge"* (Hosea 4:6). This is certainly true when it comes to our personal finances. Because of a lack of proper biblical instruction about God's way of handling money, Christians have had to resort to much of the same type of financial irresponsibility as the unsaved world.

It is this lack of knowledge that, over the years, has allowed Satan to be so effective in his deceptive practices to pervert God's original purpose regarding the use of money in the lives of Christians:

> *So he said, "I am Abraham's servant. The LORD has blessed my master abundantly, and he has become wealthy. He has given him sheep and cattle, silver and gold, menservants and maidservants, and camels and donkeys."*
> (Genesis 24:34–35 NIV)

> *Beloved, I wish above all things that thou mayest prosper and be in health, even as thy soul prospereth.* (3 John 2)

Knowledge and understanding go hand in hand. If you knew these two Scriptures but were deceived into thinking that for some reason they were not true or you did not understand how to apply them to your financial circumstances, they would be of no benefit to you. This part of your biblical inheritance would have no effect on your life. It would have no significance for your financial destiny unless you knew how to embrace it.

Yet, in addition to gaining knowledge, there is another step you must take to fulfill God's economic purposes. Once you learn the Word of God, you must be willing to act and apply it to your life.

NATURAL ACTS DETERMINE SPIRITUAL BENEFITS

Now that we know that there are certain things we must do to prepare ourselves to receive the benefits of God's provisions, let's take a closer look at what it means to take action, and what the long-term spiritual benefits of this are.

See if you can glean any significant insight from the following Scripture passage that might be helpful to us in this effort. Examine the economic circumstances that the widow of Zarephath faced:

> [Elijah] *called to her, and said, Bring me, I pray thee, a morsel of bread in thine hand. And she said, As the LORD thy God liveth, I have not a cake, but an handful of meal in a barrel, and a little oil in a cruse: and, behold, I am gathering two sticks, that I may go in and dress it for me and my son, that we may eat it, and die. And Elijah said unto her, Fear not; go and do as thou hast said: but make me thereof a little cake first, and bring it unto me, and after make for thee and for thy son. For thus saith the LORD God of Israel, The barrel of meal shall not waste, neither shall the cruse of oil fail, until the day that the LORD sendeth rain upon the earth. And she went and did according to the saying of Elijah: and she, and he, and her house, did eat many days. And the barrel of meal wasted not, neither did the cruse of oil fail, according to the word of the LORD, which he spake by Elijah.* (1 Kings 17:11–16)

If we have a word from God that can change our economic conditions, how do we apply it to our lives? From the above passage, we can see that there were already bad economic conditions in the land. The widow was down to a handful of meal when the prophet Elijah came to her. She had enough left for only one meal. But the woman's actions changed her circumstances.

By her obedience and faithfulness to do what the word of God said through Elijah, she no longer lacked anything, and her needs were met. Her circumstances changed! If the widow had not obeyed the prophet Elijah, she would not have received the blessings God had for her. She and her son would have died of starvation. However, by acting on the Word of God in obedience, she enabled God to turn her whole situation from death to life. The same is true in our lives.

This passage from 1 Kings shows us that we must not only know what the Word of God says, but we must also be obedient and act on it according to God's guidelines, in order to receive its benefits.

However, what are the actual spiritual rewards of faithfully obeying God's Word regarding our finances?

THE SPIRITUAL REWARDS

"Well done, my good servant" his master replied. "Because you have been trustworthy in a very small matter, take charge of ten cities." (Luke 19:17 NIV)

The Bible points out that there is a close correlation between skillful money management and spiritual things. This is also part of our economic inheritance. The above Scripture points out that because the steward was faithful with money, he would be given authority over cities when the master returned to establish his kingdom. Notice that this parable was told by Jesus Himself. The reward for good stewardship includes a spiritual reward to be given when Jesus returns.

The Lord was using money to illustrate this kingdom principle. The people who are faithful with the Master's money here on earth will be given authority to rule when He returns. However, another Scripture reveals that if you are not faithful with money, you won't be faithful with spiritual things: *"So if you have not been trustworthy in handling worldly wealth, who will trust you with true riches?"* (Luke 16:11 NIV).

Note another Scripture relating to money management:

His lord said unto him, Well done, thou good and faithful servant: thou hast been faithful over a few things, I will make thee ruler over many things: enter thou into the joy of thy lord. (Matthew 25:21)

In this passage, the good and faithful steward who was trustworthy with the master's money is given even more to be faithful over. However, in addition to receiving more money to manage, observe that he also is allowed to enter into the joy of the Lord.

In Luke 19 and in Matthew 25, the stewards were rewarded for being faithful with money. Each of these Scriptures also describes a spiritual reward that would be received. It is clear that there is a close correlation between faithfulness in handling money and faithfulness in handling spiritual things (Luke 16:11). Yet, the majority of families have never been able to budget their spending. Many wander aimlessly through life without ever realizing that God has attached such an importance to material possessions.

It is very important for us to realize, then, that we have an economic destiny. God has already made economic and financial provisions for His children. These provisions are available to us regardless of the condition of our finances or the condition of the economy. But because of a lack of knowledge, along with myths and traditions, many individuals, both Christian and non-Christian, don't realize how broad and nonrestrictive God's provisions are. We have been programmed to fail because of wrong attitudes.

It is also very essential for us to understand that God wants us, as Christians, to be faithful with the resources that He has already entrusted to our care. He wants us to become skillful managers of worldly wealth so that we can have a greater impact for the kingdom of God. He wants us to get our financial houses in order so that we can be in a position to reach out to others.

Finally, we should remember that in order to walk in the economic provision that God has already made available and to receive these benefits, we must be obedient to act on His Word. To survive and prosper during turbulent economic times, we need to understand that God wants us to be successful.

In the following chapters, you will find that there are basic principles that govern God's financial system and that there are many principles outlined in the Bible that give us insight into various aspects of our personal finances. However, none is more important than that of biblical stewardship, which we will discuss further in the next chapter.

PRACTICAL APPLICATION

$ Try to name at least three myths and religious traditions that would adversely affect a Christian's attitude about money and personal possessions.

$ Read the following Scriptures and answer the question, What will happen if you don't properly manage the money you have? (Matthew 25:28; Luke 16:1–2)

$ Read 1 Kings 17:11–16 and answer the question, What does it take for a Christian to receive the benefits God has provided in His Word?

CHAPTER 2

THE KEY TO SUCCESS WITH GOD

Moreover it is required in stewards, that a man be found faithful.
—1 Corinthians 4:2

Yours is the mighty power and glory and victory and majesty.
Everything in the heavens and earth is yours, O Lord, and this is
your kingdom. We adore you as being in control of everything.
Riches and honor come from you alone, and you are the Ruler of
all mankind; your hand controls power and might, and it is at
your discretion that men are made great and given strength.
—1 Chronicles 29:11–12 TLB

Things were not working out as Bob had anticipated. His wife, Sue, had gone back to work, but they were still not making ends meet. He decided to approach her about the problem. "Sue, we need to do something about these bills. I think that it's about time you stop spending all of our money on clothes. The credit card bill just came, and the charges are up again this month."

"Why didn't you think about that before you decided to buy that boat and fishing equipment?" Sue responded. "Yes, I used the charge card. I had to buy some better clothes for work. We're also spending more money on gas, lunches, and day care for the kids now. And then there's the additional car payment every month."

Bob and Sue Coleman are having marital problems stemming from difficulties in managing their personal finances. Bob earns approximately thirty thousand dollars a year as manager of a local hardware store. For the past fifteen years of marriage,

Sue's main responsibility has been to care for their three children and to manage the household.

Approximately nine months ago, Bob encouraged Sue to take a job (paying twelve thousand dollars a year) outside the home to earn extra money to buy a new car. Instead of improving the situation, however, her working seems to have caused more difficulties within the family. It appears that the family has less disposable income now than before Sue started to work.

This is a common scenario that is being played out thousands of times across the country. The average income earned by the typical American family, with both parents working, is between thirty and forty thousand dollars per year. Nevertheless, many of these families live from paycheck to paycheck, spending everything they earn just to keep afloat. I've found couples earning seventy-five thousand dollars who could not live debt-free on what they earn. The more money they earn, the more money they tend to spend. They are in financial bondage. They can't reach out to others because they are strapped themselves. Without ever realizing it, the average American family is going deeply into debt by spending more than it earns.

According to statistical data, many families are finding themselves in the same position as the Colemans. Even when both the husband and wife work, families usually find that their spending increases faster than their income. After taxes and the expenses of working, they find themselves bringing home much less money than they expected.

The key to solving this dilemma of not having enough is to understand and apply biblical stewardship to your finances. It's not the amount you have but what you do with what you have that counts. The stewardship principle is being faithful with what you have, starting where you are. As you demonstrate your faithfulness with small amounts of money, God will give you more. If you don't properly manage a small income, you won't be able to manage a larger income. Biblical stewardship is the key to success with God.

Let me repeat: the way to gain wealth in God's financial system is to start where you are and use what you have wisely. A good steward understands how money works and makes it work in his or her favor.

THE GOOD STEWARD

What does it really mean to be a good steward? True biblical stewardship, in relation to finances, is one of the most misunderstood subjects in the Bible. Again, because of the importance of finances in our lives, Satan has managed to distort our image of our true purpose as it relates to managing personal resources.

The definition of a steward is a person who manages someone else's property on behalf of the owner. The most appropriate definition of stewardship is, "faithfully applying God's principles to everything with which you have been entrusted." Good stewardship is properly managing your time, abilities, and money. It does not deal only with finances, nor does it deal only with spiritual matters. It covers everything; we will be judged in terms of what we've done with all the things that God has entrusted to our care—time, ability, and resources.

By examining the stewardship principles outlined in Matthew 25:14–30, Luke 16:1–13, and Luke 19:12–26, we are able to get true biblical insight into what God had in mind when He said, *"Good and faithful servant* [steward]*"* (Matthew 25:21). One who manages money and resources according to the principles and guidelines that God has outlined in His Word is a good steward.

The good steward is a person who increases wealth and multiplies his resources on behalf of the master. The good steward is the person who is skillful and businesslike in handling monetary affairs. The good steward is one who is faithful and diligent in carrying out the instructions given by the owner of the goods. Below is the first of many action steps to financial freedom that are highlighted throughout this book. Use them to start taking control of your finances.

Action Step

Learn to be a faithful steward over your finances.

The biggest challenge to Christians is the revelation that we will only have control of these resources for a short period of time—while we are here on earth. We are to use money as God's agent for good in the world. If we use up all that we receive on ourselves, we are mismanaging God's resources.

FAITHFULNESS WITH MATERIAL THINGS

Why is it so important for us as Christians to understand the stewardship principle? It is essential because this principle is the foundation of all other spiritual principles, and will affect our lives throughout eternity. You will be judged by your faithfulness with material things. The most important principle that we should learn as followers of Christ is biblical stewardship. This principle covers everything that we do while we are here on earth:

> *For we must all appear before the judgment seat of Christ; that every one may receive the things done in his body, according to that he hath done, whether it be good or bad.*
> (2 Corinthians 5:10)

> *Moreover it is required in stewards, that a man be found faithful.* (1 Corinthians 4:2)

Action Step

Learn how to create wealth to benefit the kingdom of God.

Again, if we are spending everything we earn on ourselves, how can we benefit the kingdom of God? The most important step in taking control of our personal finances is to learn what it means to be a steward. If we are going to be judged according to how we handle the things with which God has entrusted us here on earth, we should learn what God expects of us. We must know what God's part is and what our part is.

GOD'S PART

First, we need to recognize that God is the owner of everything. He is the God of the universe, the Creator and Supreme Ruler over the earth and everything in the earth:

Thine, O LORD, is the greatness, and the power, and the glory, and the victory, and the majesty: for all that is in the heaven and in the earth is thine; thine is the kingdom, O LORD, and thou art exalted as head above all. Both riches and honour come of thee, and thou reignest over all; and in thine hand is power and might; and in thine hand it is to make great, and to give strength unto all.

(1 Chronicles 29:11–12)

Action Step

Acknowledge God as the Owner of everything.

As we develop the right attitude about money and possessions, it is important for us to see the whole picture from an eternal perspective. As Ruler and Master, God is in control of everything on earth, and His ownership is everlasting. *"The land shall not be sold for ever: for the land is mine; for ye are strangers and sojourners with me"* (Leviticus 25:23).

The right attitude is to realize that God is owner:

For every beast of the forest is mine, and the cattle upon a thousand hills. I know all the fowls of the mountains: and the wild beasts of the field are mine. If I were hungry, I would not tell thee: for the world is mine, and the fulness thereof. (Psalm 50:10–12)

Action Step

Develop the right attitude about money and possessions.

As owner, God sets the guidelines. He makes the rules. To properly manage our money and possessions, we must learn what God expects of us. Then we must conduct the affairs of our lives according to His expectations.

Action Step

Learn what God expects of you.

Since God is owner, we must realize that we will have possessions only for a short period of time. When we pass away, all our material possessions will remain on the earth. *"For we brought nothing into this world, and it is certain we can carry nothing out"* (1 Timothy 6:7). Although we have temporary control, all these things will ultimately return to God.

Action Step

Acknowledge that everything you own while you are on earth will remain on earth.

OUR PART

Secondly, we need to recognize that we have a role to play. What does it mean to be a good steward? The Bible teaches this principle:

> *His lord said unto him, Well done, thou good and faithful servant: thou hast been faithful over a few things, I will make thee ruler over many things: enter thou into the joy of thy lord.*   (Matthew 25:21)

In order to rule over many things, you must be found faithful with what you have. In examining this parable, we can see that the master called his servants (stewards) to him and entrusted a certain amount of money to them. To one he gave five talents, to another he gave two talents, and to a third he gave one talent. He gave them his money based on their abilities. After he had entrusted them with his resources, he left them in charge. He told them to do business until he returned, and then he took his journey.

```
┌─────────────────────────────────────┐
│            Action Step              │
│                                     │
│       Be faithful with what you     │
│            already have.            │
└─────────────────────────────────────┘
```

When the master came home, he said to the first two servants, *"Well done, thou good and faithful servant:...enter thou into the joy of thy lord"* (Matthew 25:21). What did the two stewards do to deserve this type of recognition from the master? They were faithful with the master's money. The first two stewards took their lord's money and doubled it. However, the third steward took the money and buried it in the ground. To the servant who buried his money, the master said:

> *Thou wicked and slothful servant, thou knewest that I reap where I sowed not, and gather where I have not strowed: thou oughtest therefore to have put my money to the ex-changers* [banks], *and then at my coming I should have received mine own with usury* [interest]. *Take therefore the talent* [money] *from him, and give it unto him which hath ten talents. For unto every one that hath shall be given, and he shall have abundance: but from him that hath not shall be taken away even that which he hath. And cast ye the unprofitable servant into outer darkness: there shall be weeping and gnashing of teeth.* (Matthew 25:26–30)

Both of the faithful stewards doubled the money the master had given them and were given the reward. But notice that the money was taken from the third one, who had done the least. Likewise, the better you manage the money with which you have been entrusted, the more money you will have to manage.

WHAT ABOUT THE OTHER 90 PERCENT?

Many Christians are taught the practice of tithing, and they follow it religiously. This principle of giving 10 percent of our income to God is found in the Scriptures:

> *"Bring all the tithes into the storehouse, that there may be food in My house, and try Me now in this," says the LORD of hosts, "if I will not open for you the windows of heaven and pour out for you such blessing that there will not be room enough to receive it."* (Malachi 3:10 NKJV)

Tithing is an important part of God's financial system. However, many Christians believe that if they tithe, God is automatically obligated to bless their finances, without their having to follow other biblical principles regarding economics. However, the stewardship principle, as it relates to personal finances, means being faithful with all of the money that has been entrusted to you—the whole dollar, not just part of it. The stewardship principle covers more than just the 10 percent Christians give as a tithe. As we examine what it means to be a steward, we should realize that God is interested in what we do with the other 90 percent of our income, as well.

Action Step

Learn how to manage the other 90 percent of your income, after your tithe.

Unfortunately, many Christians believe that their stewardship responsibilities end after they have given their tithes and offerings on Sunday morning. During the remainder of the week, they deal with their finances pretty much as the rest of the world does, using the same financial concepts and principles. The Bible describes this as the world system: *"And be not conformed to this world: but be ye transformed by the renewing of your mind"* (Romans 12:2). Many Christians are conforming to the world system without realizing it. God wants us to learn His principles, not those of the world, and apply them to all of our personal possessions.

Remember that everything we own while we are here on earth will remain on the earth. This is a fundamental principle that God wants to get across to us. In 1 Timothy 6:17–19, the Scripture states that the gold, silver, resources, and fruits of our labors will remain in the earth and that they will do good or evil depending only on the person who is in control of them. If we, as Christians, are in control of the resources, we can use these resources to benefit the kingdom of God.

BIBLICAL PRIORITIES

What are the priorities that God outlines in His Word regarding your personal finances? *"But seek ye first the kingdom of God, and his righteousness; and all these things shall be added unto you"* (Matthew 6:33). Your first priority, then, is your individual relationship with God. This relationship must be strong before you can be successful in other relationships. All other activities are secondary. You must first seek God and His righteousness. Everything Jesus discussed while He was here on earth focused on man's relationship with God the Father. Christ relegated everything else to a lower priority.

Action Step

Get your priorities in the
proper order.

Your second priority, after God, is your relationship with your family. Your main focus should be your immediate family. The relationship between husband and wife is first. Then comes the relationship between parent and child. We should care for our families and make sure our children understand the spiritual side of the Gospel. We should point our children in the right direction: *"Train up a child in the way he should go: and when he is old, he will not depart from it"* (Proverbs 22:6). This principle will be discussed further in chapter 11.

Your third priority is your profession or business. The third priority takes into account how you earn a living, what your professional and business activities are. How we earn the money we have and what we are willing to do to get the money says a lot about our spiritual condition.

God is first, our families are second, and our professions or businesses are third. We must always give each of these areas the right priority in our lives.

HOW TO RECEIVE MORE MONEY

If your income is small, how do you get more money? One way is to develop new and creative ideas for generating income according to the gifts and talents God has given you. However, just increasing your income isn't the answer. You have to learn how to manage your resources well. According to the stewardship principle described in Matthew 25, even if God gave you an entrepreneurial idea that helped to double, triple, or otherwise multiply your income, your seeming financial success would cause you more harm than good if you didn't manage your money well.

The stewardship principle teaches us that our primary responsibility is to be faithful with what we have: *"For unto every one that hath shall be given, and he shall have abundance: but from him that hath not shall be taken away even that which he hath"* (Matthew 25:29).

Action Step

Be faithful with the money with which God has entrusted you: learn how to make it grow.

Remember that being faithful with what we have is the key aspect of the stewardship principle as it relates to personal finances. Being faithful with what we have is the prerequisite for receiving more in the future. If we don't take care of the resources we have, God will not bless us with additional resources in the future.

The steward who was not faithful with what he was given had his money taken away from him. Look back at the first part of Matthew 25:29: *"For unto every one that hath shall be given."* A close examination of the whole verse reveals that it could easily be read, "Everyone who is faithful with what he has will be given more and will have an abundance. However, regarding the one who is not faithful, even what he has will be taken away." Lack of knowledge of this principle is part of the reason we see so much economic decay in our urban centers. Most people don't understand how to apply the basic principle of stewardship!

Action Step

Use it, or you will lose it.

The only thing that will count for eternity is what we have done for the kingdom of God—how we have used the resources that God has provided to benefit the kingdom. Yet, too many Christians are living from day to day. They don't have any resources left with which to help anyone else. They spend all of their working time trying to make a living for themselves and their families. They genuinely love God, but they are struggling just to make ends meet. They have to believe God for a miracle just to pay their electric bills.

Many Christians are like Bob and Sue Coleman, whom I mentioned at the beginning of the chapter. They are members of small churches that reach out to the community. They would like to give more money to their churches; however, because of their financial circumstances, they don't have anything to give. They are using all the financial resources God has given them on themselves. Consequently, they are having no impact for His kingdom.

PRACTICAL APPLICATION

$ After reading this chapter, identify steps that you can take to be a more effective steward of the resources with which God has entrusted you.

$ Commit the following Scripture to memory: *"The earth is the LORD's, and the fulness thereof; the world, and they that dwell therein"* (Psalm 24:1). Memorizing this Scripture will remind you that God is really the true Owner of all things, and you are only the steward of what He has given you. Your success will be based on how well you manage the Lord's property while you are here on earth.

CHAPTER 3

PLANNING AND PREPARATION

*A prudent man foresees the difficulties ahead and prepares for
them; the simpleton goes blindly on and
suffers the consequences.*
—Proverbs 22:3 TLB

*Any enterprise is built by wise planning, becomes strong through
common sense, and profits wonderfully
by keeping abreast of the facts.*
—Proverbs 24:3–4 TLB

*But don't begin until you count the cost. For who would begin
construction of a building without first getting estimates and
then checking to see if he has enough money to pay the bills?*
—Luke 14:28 TLB

It has been approximately two years since John and Janet
Jones were shocked into reality. John was laid off from the
job that he had held for the past twenty-five years. The
company for which he worked merged with another corporation.
As a result, John lost his job.

John and Janet had thought that because this company had
been around for seventy-five years, John had a secure job. With
an annual bonus and profit sharing, John realized he was receiving an annual salary well above what he could get on the
current job market. It would be difficult for him to find a com-
parable position.

John had learned from his father that one should always
put "a little something" aside for the future. Although he had
put some savings in a mutual fund, over the years he and Janet

had been taken captive by the trappings of the good life. They had thought that financial ruin could never happen to them. However, because of the severity of their situation, they were forced to sell their home and drastically alter their lifestyle.

Initially, it was disaster for Janet when they moved into an apartment. She never thought they could survive on the $1,000 per month they had from a mutual fund investment. For the first time in their lives, they were forced to budget their income. They cut back on spending and set realistic priorities based on their current income. In their apartment, the utility bills were less than a third of what they had been paying. They now conducted all business transactions on a cash basis. Fancy clothes, eating out, and entertainment were eliminated. They sold most of their furniture. They took drastic measures to conserve money to bring their expenses in line with their income. Suddenly, they realized that they could live on much less than they had thought.

The Joneses had implemented one of the basic principles of God's financial system: always set aside a portion of your income. They would eventually recover from the setback because they had set aside a portion of their income for emergencies and had enough discipline to drastically restructure their lifestyle. They realized that, in our economy, no job is forever. They also realized that they could live on a lot less money than they had been living on just two years earlier.

How to Develop a Surplus

Your first goal in becoming free from financial bondage is to learn how to develop a surplus. This process is easy once you learn how God's financial system operates. If you spend less than you take in, you will always have a surplus. What to do with this surplus will be discussed in greater detail in chapter 8, which deals with saving and investing.

Many Christians feel that after they have given a tithe (10 percent) or offering to God's work, their spiritual responsibility is over, as far as money is concerned. This is not what the Bible teaches. God is interested in how we handle the whole dollar, not just part of it. If you don't properly handle the other 90 percent, you will never have a surplus.

As stewards, we are responsible for 100 percent of everything that has been entrusted to our care. We must revise our thinking to take into account that we are stewards over all the money the Lord has given us. We will be held accountable if we waste God's resources.

And he said also unto his disciples, There was a certain rich man, which had a steward; and the same was accused unto him that he had wasted his goods. And he called him, and said unto him, How is it that I hear this of thee? give an account of thy stewardship; for thou mayest be no longer steward. (Luke 16:1–2)

This Scripture points out the results of wastefulness in relation to money. Each Christian should be interested in getting as much mileage as possible from every dime of every dollar. With this in mind, we must ask ourselves how to handle the other part of our incomes after we give. In other words, we need to examine what we are doing with the other 90 percent.

HOW TO DEVELOP YOUR ECONOMIC POTENTIAL

A good steward knows how money works and plans for the future. Planning ahead helps you to walk in your full economic potential. It allows you to prepare yourself to be able to meet the conditions that God has put forth in His Word.

Once God tells you to do something through His Word, it is not always possible for you to do it right then. Planning ahead allows you to get in a position where you can be obedient to do what God's Word says to do. This is especially true when it comes to your personal finances.

The purpose of this chapter is to help you organize a plan to manage the whole dollar so that you can get the maximum benefit from every dollar that God has entrusted to your care.

BEING A GOOD STEWARD OVER THE WHOLE DOLLAR

The majority of individuals spend 100 percent of their money without taking God into account. If every Christian gives 10 percent before taxes to carry out the work of the Gospel, he or she has 90 percent left to cover other expenditures. Yet, most Christians, once they give to God's work, use the same practices that non-Christians use to determine how they will spend the balance of their money. For the most part, they are ending up with the same disastrous results.

To take control of your finances, you must look at your total income from a different perspective. You must take control of each dollar and tell it which direction it should go. The first step in this process is to develop a budget; we will examine this in detail later in the chapter. But first, let's take a look at what the Scriptures say about planning ahead.

GOD'S ATTITUDE ABOUT PLANNING AHEAD

Planning ahead gives us the ability to look into the future and see our desires fulfilled. It helps us to close the gap between hope and reality. It is the natural bridge that can lead us from where we are in the present to where God wants us to be in the future.

Planning and preparation are fundamental principles that are outlined in the Bible and that will have a definite impact on your personal finances. Once you have identified the biblical guidelines for managing your finances, it will be necessary for you to prepare a plan of action to accomplish your goals.

Action Step

Believe that God has established
guidelines that allow you to
properly plan your financial affairs,
no matter how much
money you earn.

There are many Scriptures in the Bible that point to the fact that we should plan our actions. Planning is key for success with God:

Any enterprise is built by wise planning, becomes strong through common sense, and profits wonderfully by keeping abreast of the facts. (Proverbs 24:3–4 TLB)

Suppose one of you wants to build a tower. Will he not first sit down and estimate the cost to see if he has enough money to complete it? (Luke 14:28 NIV)

Write the vision and make it plain on tablets, that he may run who reads it. (Habakkuk 2:2 NKJV)

Where there is no vision, the people perish: but he that keepeth the law, happy is he. (Proverbs 29:18)

In examining these Scriptures, we should note that God Himself planned ahead. He made preparations for the plan of salvation before He created the world. He looked forward into the future and saw Jesus crucified on the cross. Then He worked backward to establish steps in His plan of redemption, with Jesus' obedience clearly in sight. God always plans ahead.

In 1 Corinthians 14:40, the Scripture states, *"Everything should be done in a fitting and orderly way"* (NIV). God is a God of planning and organization. Note that before Jesus ascended to the Father, He told the disciples that He was going to prepare a place for them in heaven. The Scripture reads:

There are many homes up there where my Father lives, and I am going to prepare them for your coming. When everything is ready, then I will come and get you, so that you can always be with me where I am. If this weren't so, I would tell you plainly. (John 14:2–3 TLB)

There are some other notable examples of planning and preparation in the Bible:

Noah was another who trusted God. When he heard God's warning about the future, Noah believed him even though there was then no sign of a flood, and wasting no time, he built the ark and saved his family. Noah's belief in God was in direct contrast to the sin and disbelief of the rest of the world—which refused to obey—and because of his faith he became one of those whom God has accepted.
(Hebrews 11:7 TLB)

49

Observe the sequence. Noah received a word from God, and then he began to prepare in line with God's plan. Another example is David's preparation for building the temple:

"Solomon my son is young and tender," David said, "and the Temple of the Lord must be a marvelous structure, famous and glorious throughout the world; so I will begin the preparations for it now." So David collected the construction materials before his death.

(1 Chronicles 22:5 TLB)

Action Step

Always plan your financial affairs:
don't allow them to happen
haphazardly.

We can see from the following Scripture that King Hezekiah was instructed to prepare for his death. A wise steward plans ahead.

In those days was Hezekiah sick unto death. And the prophet Isaiah the son of Amoz came to him, and said unto him, Thus saith the LORD, Set thine house in order; for thou shalt die, and not live.   (2 Kings 20:1)

God also used Moses' father-in-law to give Moses good advice on organizing and governing the people of Israel:

Find some capable, godly, honest men who hate bribes, and appoint them as judges, one judge for each 1,000 people; he in turn will have ten judges under him, each in charge of a hundred; and under each of them will be two judges, each responsible for the affairs of fifty people; and each of these will have five judges beneath him, each counseling ten persons.   (Exodus 18:21 TLB)

In addition, the Lord spoke to Moses and gave him the plans for building the tabernacle:

This home of mine shall be a tent pavilion—a Tabernacle.
I will give you a drawing of the construction plan and the
details of each furnishing.   (Exodus 25:9 TLB)

Notice in the last two Scriptures that detailed instructions
were given ahead of time in order to accomplish something.

HOW TO SUBSTANTIALLY INCREASE YOUR INCOME

For the average family, each dollar can be divided roughly
into three categories: one-third taxes, one-third interest and insurance, and one-third that usually goes to pay debt as well as
living expenses. Once the bills are paid, there is nothing left for
emergencies or the things of God.

By setting financial goals, establishing a budget, and planning ahead, you can substantially increase your disposable income (fig. 1). Our goal in this chapter is to examine the biblical
principle of planning as it relates to reducing the spending categories that rob the average Christian of disposable income.

FIGURE 1
Disposable Income (After Tithe and Savings)

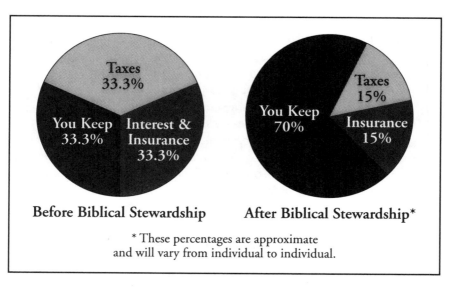

Before Biblical Stewardship   After Biblical Stewardship*

* These percentages are approximate
and will vary from individual to individual.

**Figure 1 shows your income before and after applying biblical
guidelines for managing money.**

How to Live on 70 Percent of Your Income

This section will help you examine ways to allocate the other 90 percent of your income, after your tithe. First of all, set a goal to live on 70 percent of your income. At first this might seem absolutely impossible, especially to those individuals who are having problems living on 100 percent of what they already earn. Even though it may seem impossible, let's take a closer look at this concept.

If you could realign your current finances so that you only spent 70 percent of each paycheck, what would this do for your personal finances? First, you would put yourself in a position where you could systematically take into account every financial principle described in the Bible.

Action Step

Organize your financial planning
and goals according to biblical
guidelines.

Joseph followed this basic pattern:

Let Pharaoh do this, and let him appoint officers over the land, and take up the fifth part [20 percent] of the land of Egypt in the seven plenteous years. And let them gather all the food of those good years that come, and lay up corn under the hand of Pharaoh, and let them keep food in the cities. And that food shall be for store to the land against the seven years of famine, which shall be in the land of Egypt; that the land perish not through the famine.

(Genesis 41:34–36)

Notice that Joseph recommended to Pharaoh that he take a fifth part, 20 percent, and set it aside. In other words, he recommended that the Egyptians set aside 20 percent when the resources were coming in so that they would have resources when hard times came. Even though the Egyptians did not tithe, we know that Joseph was a wise steward and understood the tithing principle.

Action Step

Set a goal to live on 70 percent of your income.

The same pattern is evident in Proverbs 6:6–8. According to this Scripture, the ants were wise because they set aside resources in the summer so that they would have provisions in the winter. This is not a biblical law, but it is a biblical pattern.

Therefore, living on 70 percent of your income would allow you to begin to put into practice biblical principles for finances. Secondly, living on 70 percent would give you a 30 percent surplus, including the first 10 percent to give to God's work. You would be putting God in first place. Finally, having a surplus would provide a steady source of revenue for your short-term and long-term savings accounts.

Action Step

Establish your savings and investments in a way that is consistent with biblical guidelines.

For example, if you were to set aside 10 percent for short-term savings, you would have a surplus account that could be used to extend a helping hand to those around you. You could give to the poor and needy and still have enough to purchase the things you need. You would have enough resources to carry you through unforeseen emergencies and repairs, to cover insurance deductibles, or even to be able to pay cash for new purchases.

If you were also to set aside 10 percent for long-term savings, you would be in a position to plan ahead for retirement. You wouldn't have to depend on the government when you retired. Compound interest would be working for you instead of against you. According to the Scriptures, you would be in a position to lend and not borrow; you would be the head, not the tail (Deuteronomy 28:12–13).

Please take note that the 10 percent for long- and short-term savings is just an example and a goal to aim for. You may not be in a position to save this amount at the present time, but you should set aside something.

If you were to set a goal of living on 70 percent, it would change the entire complexion of your existing financial picture. Your goal would be to reorganize your spending habits so that you could live on a maximum of 70 percent of your income after you developed a surplus. Under this new arrangement, the outgoing expense chart would look like Figure 2.

Figure 2
Outgoing Expenditures
Your Budgetary Dollar

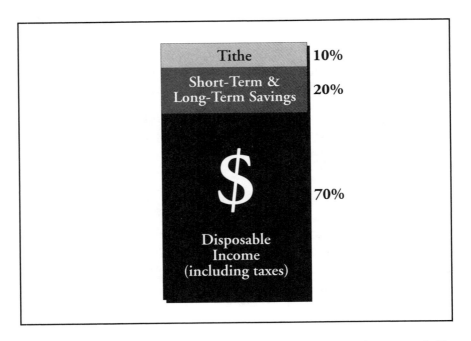

Figure 2 shows your budget with outgoing spending under control. By setting a goal to live on 70 percent of your income, you would have a 20 percent surplus.

If you were to set aside 20 percent of your disposable income (after your tithe) in a surplus account, you would have 70 percent to spend on taxes and monthly living expenses. This would mean that you would automatically be living within your means because you would be forcing monthly expenditures to fit in the guidelines you will have established.

By setting a goal to live on 70 percent, you would manage the whole dollar, not just part of it. You would be in a position to live above the ups and downs of the economy. You wouldn't be at the mercy of your employer. You would never again have "more month than money."

ALWAYS SPEND LESS THAN YOU EARN

Planning ahead is essential if you are to be a good steward and a good giver. You don't have to spend everything you earn to be a good Christian. Satan has misled many Christians into thinking it is unspiritual to have a savings account or money set aside for emergencies or investments. They feel it shows an overall lack of trust in God's provision. As we have seen in this chapter, this is completely contrary to Scripture. As an investment banker working with individual and institutional finances, I have seen this attitude cause havoc in families and the nation as a whole.

In this chapter, we have seen that the Bible clearly establishes the principle of planning ahead and setting aside a portion of one's income for future needs. The Scriptures indicate in Proverbs 6:6–8 and Proverbs 21:20 that a person who stores up in time of plenty and prepares for the winter is wise.

If you spend less than you earn, you will always have a surplus or savings account. A key to your financial future is to discipline yourself to set aside a portion of your income each month on a consistent basis and cut your expenses so that if something unforeseen should happen or when God moves on your heart to do something for His kingdom, you won't be restrained by your financial circumstances.

CHAPTER 4

DEALING WITH THE BONDAGE OF DEBT

The rich ruleth over the poor, and the borrower
is servant to the lender.
—Proverbs 22:7

Love not the world, neither the things that are in the world. If
any man love the world, the love of the Father is not in him. For
all that is in the world, the lust of the flesh, and the lust of the
eyes, and the pride of life, is not of the Father,
but is of the world.
—1 John 2:15–16

L arry and Connie are pastors of a church with a large membership. "I think the worst mistake we made was when the church decided to borrow money from the members," Larry told me.

I listened as the story unfolded. Larry had been in the ministry for twenty years. For the last fifteen years, his church had experienced tremendous growth. During that time, he had also started a successful Christian school in addition to overseeing his church ministry. Because of the growth, he decided to expand his facilities.

"The expansion seemed like a simple thing to me, since we were taking in enough money to meet the payments when we were in a smaller building," Larry continued. "I decided to move forward with the planned construction of a larger church. To secure financing, we had to use the school and the ministry's other property as collateral for the land and new facilities.

"Everything seemed to be going okay until a major plant closed in our area. The income of the church dropped tremendously. If we don't come up with some way of paying the monthly note, the lenders are threatening to foreclose. We could lose both the church and school, as well as the money some of the members lent the church," Larry said.

SURETY, THE IMPROPER USE OF DEBT

Larry and Connie's situation illustrates another principle that governs success or failure in God's financial system: the principle of surety, or the improper use of debt. A person will never be able to become totally free financially if he or she cannot control spending.

This is a tragic case, but such situations occur more times than you can imagine for individuals and businesses alike. When a person incurs debt to finance a new purchase and has to risk existing assets to secure the loan, this is called *surety,* and God has much to say in the Bible about such activities.

One-third of the income of the average family goes toward debt principal and interest payments. This chapter is designed to help you understand how surety works and the power that debt has over our lives.

HOW DEBT TAKES CONTROL

The seed of financial problems is normally planted early in children's lives, when they observe the actions of their parents. Many children are never taught the basics of how to handle money. As they grow up, they feel that they immediately should have everything that their parents took a lifetime to acquire.

Action Step

Determine that you will never put furniture, clothes, or personal items on a credit card or charge account.

The average young family starts off by purchasing an automobile, furniture, and clothing on credit. This starts a debt pattern that usually sets the tone for the rest of their lives. Once this cycle is set into motion, it is not easily broken. By the time the first items are paid for, the couple usually finds something else that they feel is needed. Gradually, their income becomes consumed by interest and monthly payments.

Once the credit card company provides easier access to credit with higher ceilings and lower minimum payments, the cycle is almost complete. The grip of debt is tightened, and this often leads to the destruction of personal integrity, bankruptcy, and even the breakup of the family.

Action Step

Pay off your credit cards in full
each month or cut them up.

WHAT IS DEBT?

Here is the basic definition of debt: an individual or corporation makes a commitment to purchase a product or service and agrees to pay the obligation in the future. This obligation normally takes the form of principal and interest payments.

However, debt is much more than monthly payments. People can fall into a spirit of debt. When debt gets out of control, it can render you useless to the kingdom of God. It becomes your master. It can weaken the basic foundation of the average family. It comes as a result of greed and lack of self-control, and it is usually accompanied by improper financial planning or no planning at all.

Action Step

Acknowledge that God wants you
out of debt.

Debt is a thief. It robs us of our time and money. Debt causes worry and anxiety. Debt causes conflict with family members and friends. Debt destroys our Christian witness. It prevents us from being a blessing to God and others. In most cases, when we become bogged down in debt, our attention turns inward to personal problems. We spend most of our time trying to earn money just to meet our obligations. There is no money left to help someone who might be in need. We are held in bondage. In too many cases, we are captured by the stronghold of debt for a whole lifetime without even realizing it.

WHAT DOES GOD'S WORD SAY ABOUT DEBT?

Exercising patience is critical in breaking the stronghold of debt. As Christians, we should be very careful about making commitments that bind us to do something in the future that might conflict with what God has planned for our lives.

The Bible is quite clear about the subject of debt and surety. Debt falls under the general guidelines of borrowing and lending. Borrowing money, in itself, is not a sin, but God's Word has much to say about surety—making promises and obligating your future time and resources.

Action Step

Examine the consequences before making a commitment of your time or money.

In examining what the Bible says about debt, we must note that in addition to the general categories of borrowing and lending, anytime we observe the terms *usury, trust, vows, cosigning, striking hands,* and *surety,* the Bible is referring to debt in one form or another.

The Bible teaches that the person who borrows puts himself or herself in servitude to debt: *"The rich ruleth over the poor, and the borrower is servant* [slave] *to the lender"* (Proverbs 22:7). This is certainly true. A person who is heavily involved in debt is a slave to his or her debts in both time and money. This Scripture also points out that if debt is not used properly, it will ultimately keep that individual poor. By its very nature, debt requires the transfer of wealth from the borrower to the lender, from one individual to another. The apostle Paul wrote, *"Owe no man any thing, but to love one another"* (Romans 13:8), and, *"Ye are bought with a price; be not ye the servants of men"* (1 Corinthians 7:23).

The main thing, however, is that God doesn't want us so bogged down in the whole economic system that we can't do His will on the earth with our lives.

> *Love not the world, neither the things that are in the world. If any man love the world, the love of the Father is not in him. For all that is in the world, the lust of the flesh, and the lust of the eyes, and the pride of life, is not of the Father, but is of the world.* (1 John 2:15–16)

HOW TO DOUBLE THE MONEY YOU KEEP

By following biblical guidelines regarding debt, you can increase your financial resources. As I pointed out earlier, the income of the average family may be divided roughly into three categories: one-third for taxes, one-third for interest and insurance, and one-third for spending, usually for principal payments (see figure 1, chapter 3). This kind of arrangement will only lead to debt and frustration. The Bible tells us:

> *Ye have sown much, and bring in little; ye eat, but ye have not enough; ye drink, but ye are not filled with drink; ye clothe you, but there is none warm; and he that earneth wages earneth wages to put it into a bag with holes.*
> (Haggai 1:6)

To take control of your personal finances, you must learn to manage all three of these categories, but perhaps the most important area is debt. Most families can more than double their income by simply eliminating principal and interest payments.

By establishing a budget and planning ahead (see figures 4 and 5, chapter 9), you can substantially increase your disposable income. That is why, in the chapters that follow, I will show you how to reduce interest, insurance, and tax payments so that you can have more spendable income.

FIGURE 3
Increase in Disposable Income

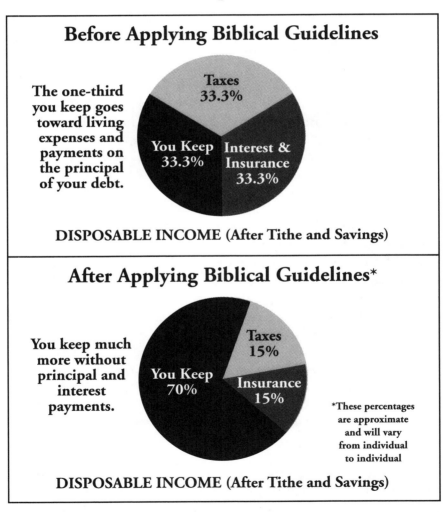

Before Applying Biblical Guidelines

The one-third you keep goes toward living expenses and payments on the principal of your debt.

Taxes 33.3%

You Keep 33.3%

Interest & Insurance 33.3%

DISPOSABLE INCOME (After Tithe and Savings)

After Applying Biblical Guidelines*

You keep much more without principal and interest payments.

Taxes 15%

You Keep 70%

Insurance 15%

*These percentages are approximate and will vary from individual to individual

DISPOSABLE INCOME (After Tithe and Savings)

Figure 3 shows the increase in disposable income that the average family can gain by eliminating debt principal and interest payments.

> ## Action Step
>
> Establish a debt-reduction plan immediately to reduce principal and interest payments.

The debt-reduction plan in this chapter can enable the typical family to be completely debt free and earning interest income to build wealth in approximately five years or less. However, before we focus on debt reduction, let's take a closer look at the great impact that debt is having on our lives.

THE POWER OF DEBT

Debt has become a serious problem in our country over the past twenty years. It can be divided into three major categories:

1. National debt
2. Corporate debt
3. Personal debt

To understand the magnitude of the debt problem, let's examine these three aspects.

National Debt

The federal government is the major debtor. Because of overspending, our country has moved from being the number one creditor nation to the world's largest debtor nation in a matter of a few years. Our national debt is over five trillion dollars. The interest on our national debt is almost equivalent to what we spend for defense, more than 15 percent of total national expenditures. And the country is rapidly coming to the point where it will not be able to collect enough taxes to pay the interest on the national debt. This, of course, would bankrupt our economy.

Corporate Debt

The '80s were known as the decade of mergers and acquisitions. Many of our bedrock corporations, in an effort to grow and expand their influence, purchased smaller subsidiaries using worthless junk bonds. As a result, many of our best-known and strongest corporations have been burdened with excessive debt.

Personal Debt

Personal debt takes the form of home, automobile, furniture, department store, and, of course, credit card purchases. With personal debt, we notice the same trend as in government and corporate debt. Individual borrowing also has increased at an alarming rate. The world system has completely indoctrinated Christians and non-Christians alike into thinking it is impossible to live in our society without being deeply in debt. Because of the Wall Street and Madison Avenue mentalities, many individuals have found themselves making purchases that far exceed their ability to repay. As a result, many families are only one paycheck away from total financial disaster.

IN THE OLD TESTAMENT, DEBT IS A CURSE

Regarding the principle of borrowing and lending, the Scriptures state:

> *And it shall come to pass, if thou shalt hearken diligently unto the voice of the LORD thy God, to observe and to do all his commandments which I command thee this day, that the LORD thy God will set thee on high above all nations of the earth: and all these blessings shall come on thee, and overtake thee, if thou shalt hearken unto the voice of the LORD thy God....Thou shalt lend unto many nations, and thou shalt not borrow.* (Deuteronomy 28:1–2, 12)

> *But it shall come to pass, if thou wilt not hearken unto the voice of the LORD thy God, to observe to do all his commandments and his statutes which I command thee this*

day; that all these curses shall come upon thee, and over-
take thee....The stranger that is within thee shall get up
above thee very high; and thou shalt come down very low.
He shall lend to thee, and thou shalt not lend to him: he
shall be the head, and thou shalt be the tail.
(Deuteronomy 28:15, 43–44)

This warning has certainly come to pass in our country and in the lives of many families. They are the tail and not the head because they did not listen to God's Word regarding debt.

Another important aspect of debt is that it makes a presumption on the future. It presumes, first of all, that you will have the money to pay the obligation. Secondly, it presumes that you will be alive to meet the debt. However, the Scriptures say,

Go to now, ye that say, To day or to morrow we will go into
such a city, and continue there a year, and buy and sell,
and get gain: whereas ye know not what shall be on the
morrow. For what is your life? It is even a vapour, that ap-
peareth for a little time, and then vanisheth away. For that
ye ought to say, If the Lord will, we shall live, and do this,
or that.   (James 4:13–15)

FINANCIAL FREEDOM GOD'S WAY

According to Deuteronomy 28:44, God expects you to be the head and not the tail. Under the borrowing and lending principle, the Bible indicates that you should be the lender, not the borrower. This implies that you should have money to lend and be in a position to extend loans and give to others. As a Christian, this is part of your economic destiny. Notice the picture that the following Scriptures paint:

He who has pity on the poor lends to the LORD, and He
will pay back what he has given.   (Proverbs 19:17 NKJV)

But love ye your enemies, and do good, and lend, hoping
for nothing again; and your reward shall be great, and ye

*shall be the children of the Highest: for he is kind unto the
unthankful and to the evil.*   (Luke 6:35)

*Give to him that asketh thee, and from him that would
borrow of thee turn not thou away.*   (Matthew 5:42)

He is ever merciful, and lendeth; and his seed is blessed.
                                                  (Psalm 37:26)

*A good man showeth favour, and lendeth: he will guide
his affairs with discretion.*   (Psalm 112:5)

God wants us to have enough of a surplus to lend and give to
others.

Action Step

Set a goal to have a surplus account.

LET INTEREST WORK FOR YOU, NOT AGAINST YOU

Is it acceptable for Christians to receive interest on their
money? The Bible states that there are certain times when interest can be charged, and there are other times when interest
should not be charged:

*If thou lend money to any of my people that is poor by thee,
thou shalt not be to him as an usurer, neither shalt thou
lay upon him usury.*   (Exodus 22:25)

*If one of your brethren becomes poor, and falls into poverty
among you, then you shall help him, like a stranger or a
sojourner, that he may live with you. Take no usury or interest from him; but fear your God, that your brother may
live with you.*   (Leviticus 25:35–36 NKJV)

*Thou shalt not lend upon usury to thy brother; usury of
money, usury of victuals, usury of any thing that is lent
upon usury.*   (Deuteronomy 23:19)

Action Step

Use interest to benefit the kingdom
of God.

There are certain cases, however, in which it's okay to charge interest. As a matter of fact, God implemented the principle of interest. The Bible normally refers to it as *usury:*

> *Unto a stranger thou mayest lend upon usury; but unto thy brother thou shalt not lend upon usury: that the LORD thy God may bless thee in all that thou settest thine hand to in the land whither thou goest to possess it.*
> (Deuteronomy 23:20)

In this Scripture, we have two categories of lending—to a stranger and to a brother. The word *brother* refers to a member of an individual's household or a fellow Jew. The Bible tells us it is all right to charge interest. A Christian should be a wise manager and skillful investor, acting as a wise steward over all the resources that have been entrusted to him or her. A good steward realizes that one hundred thousand dollars invested at 20 percent interest will produce the same income as working all year for twenty thousand dollars. A good steward plans ahead according to God's guidelines.

Action Step

Always pay all debts you
have created.

A Christian also should be a wise steward of anything he or she has borrowed from another. Regarding the repayment of debt, the Scriptures state that if a man borrows anything from his neighbor and the property is damaged or destroyed, the borrower must fully compensate for the loss: *"If a man borrows an animal from his neighbor and it is injured or dies while the owner is not present, he must make restitution"* (Exodus 22:14 NIV).

WHAT ABOUT SURETY?

The Bible tells us that we should avoid putting ourselves in a position of surety. Surety is security against loss, damage, or failure to do something. The dictionary definition of *surety* is agreeing to be legally responsible for the debt, default, or conduct of someone else. The biblical definition of *surety* is making a debt or commitment without having a sure way to repay the debt (collateral worth more than the debt), whether it is for yourself or someone else. Notice what the Scriptures say about surety:

Be not thou one of them that strike hands, or of them that are sureties for debts. (Proverbs 22:26)

A man devoid of understanding shakes hands in a pledge, And becomes surety for his friend. (Proverbs 17:18 NKJV)

He who puts up security for another will surely suffer, but whoever refuses to strike hands in pledge is safe. (Proverbs 11:15 NIV)

My son, if thou be surety for thy friend, if thou hast stricken thy hand with a stranger, thou art snared with the words of thy mouth, thou art taken with the words of thy mouth. Do this now, my son, and deliver thyself, when thou art come into the hand of thy friend; go, humble thyself, and make sure thy friend. Give not sleep to thine eyes, nor slumber to thine eyelids. Deliver thyself as a roe from the hand of the hunter, and as a bird from the hand of the fowler. (Proverbs 6:1–5)

Action Step

Learn what it means to be in a surety position, and then don't allow yourself to be trapped.

A good example of surety is when you purchase a new car (the collateral) and the debt for which you obligated yourself is more than the market value of your car. If the automobile were worth enough to cover the debt, you would not be putting yourself in a surety position. Suppose you bought the automobile for ten thousand dollars with a down payment of two thousand dollars, and for some reason you could not meet the monthly payments for the balance of eight thousand dollars. If the car (the collateral) were picked up and the debt canceled, then you would not be in a surety position. The automobile would be collateral sufficient to satisfy the debt. You would have a sure way to pay. On the other hand, if the lender were to repossess the automobile and you still owed the balance of the debt, you would be in a surety position.

The same can be true for real estate transactions. Suppose you bought a duplex apartment, appraised at one hundred thousand dollars, for which the bank agreed to lend you eighty thousand dollars. Since you would have the building as collateral for the debt, you would not be putting yourself in a surety position. If something should happen to prevent your paying the monthly note and the bank repossessed the building, you would lose your down payment of twenty thousand dollars, but you would not be obligated to pay the balance. Then you would not be in a surety position. The building would serve as collateral for itself. There would be a sure way to repay the loan. However, if, for some reason, you can't pay a bill, the lender repossesses the collateral, and you have to tap other resources to pay the balance of the debt, you are in a surety position.

DECEPTIVE SURETY

Unfortunately, many families are in a surety position and don't realize it. For decades, the real estate market was increasing in value, and you could always sell your home for a price that was higher than what you paid. In recent years, however, with real estate prices decreasing, many people have found themselves in a home that is actually worth less on the market than the balance they owe. They are in a surety position.

Action Step

Examine your home, assets, and
business to see if you are
in a surety position.

The best way to avoid a surety position on your home, car, or business is with a sufficient down payment. Where there is a sufficiently high amount of equity involved, surety is usually avoided. If the lending institution agrees to receive the property as full payment for the debt in case something should go wrong, you have a sure way to repay the loan. You are not in a surety position.

With credit cards, you are extremely vulnerable to surety. You should pay your credit card debt in full at the end of each month. If you don't have the money to pay the balance owed in full, you should not use the card because you would be breaking the surety principle.

Business surety is causing big problems in the United States. As an investment banker, I have had the opportunity to see many business transactions involving a great amount of debt. Debt is a tool like any other financial instrument, but if it is not used properly, it can cause tremendous problems for a business.

A certain amount of risk is involved in any business. There are many businesspeople who take calculated risks with a portion of their income as an investment to receive a future return on their money. However, there are other businesspeople who are constantly betting their entire futures and businesses on "one roll of the dice"—that one major business deal. In essence, what they are doing is going into surety, using resources that they have already accumulated as collateral to borrow on the future. What would happen if a particular project should fail? The businessperson would lose the money he or she has already accumulated, plus the current business, not to mention his or her reputation. Such a person would have to start over, often losing his or her life's savings and disrupting the lives of the employees of the business in the process.

Action Step

Determine never to put all your
eggs in one basket.

COMMITMENTS ARE SERIOUS TO GOD

The biggest problem we have in the area of debt and surety
is that of commitment. Joshua made a commitment to live in
peace with certain kings (Joshua 9:1–20). Although he was deceived because the kings lied to him, Joshua had to live up to
the commitments that he had made. He had to follow through,
even though his commitments caused him great difficulties
later.

As Christians, we should never put ourselves in a surety
position. Even in the best of times, we must be careful never to
"put all our eggs in one basket." We should never risk a business or life's savings on any one project. As good stewards, according to Luke 14:28, we must examine the outcome and
count the cost before the commitment is made. *"For which of
you, intending to build a tower, sitteth not down first, and
counteth the cost, whether he have sufficient to finish it?"*
(Luke 14:28).

We should never make a commitment beyond our ability to
pay; instead, we must be sure that we can follow through on our
obligations. We should examine all areas of the obligation prior
to making a long-term commitment of time or money. The consequences of our commitments always need to be examined, and
any obligation we make should be in harmony with biblical
guidelines.

Action Step

Count the cost, and refuse to make
a hasty decision where debt or
investments are involved.

WHEN LIABILITIES ARE GREATER THAN ASSETS

Another condition of surety that is often misunderstood is when an individual's liabilities are greater than his or her assets (when a person's debt is greater than the market value of what he or she owns). This is typical of a person who is overspending his or her salary. If a person is earning two thousand dollars per month but is spending twenty-two hundred per month, he or she is already in a surety position or is rapidly approaching it. Because the average family does not keep records, people often are unaware that they are spending more money than they take in by charging things on their credit cards. These debts usually accumulate over a period of time and ultimately cause serious financial problems.

One way to determine if you are in an overall surety position is to total the value of all your assets. If the total debt you owe on your assets exceeds the current market value for them, you are already in a surety position. If you were to liquidate your assets, you would not have a way to pay the balance of your debt. In essence, you would have to count on future earnings to pay your obligation.

FIVE WAYS TO BREAK THE POWER OF DEBT

Remember that the borrower is in bondage to debt. According to Proverbs 22:7, *"the borrower is servant to the lender."* God wants us to be debt-free, to have a surplus, and to be able to lend instead of borrow.

If you are trapped by the debt cycle, what do you do? How do you get out when you are in over your head? It takes discipline. However, once you know what to look for, you can focus on the solution. There are five practical steps that you can take to break the power of debt in your life, get your financial house in order, and live above your financial circumstances.

Ask God to Break the Power

First, you must make a firm commitment to break the power of debt in your life. Ask God to give you the strength, wisdom, and discipline to become debt-free.

Stop Buying Things on Credit

Secondly, you must stop purchasing things on credit. This will be the most difficult step to take after you make a firm commitment. Put all credit cards and charge accounts on hold. To have victory over debt, you must stop buying things on credit. Stop all deficit spending. Instead of using credit cards, use cash. If you don't have the money, do without. Never spend more money than you take in.

Start a Debt-Reduction Plan

Thirdly, begin implementation of a debt-reduction plan immediately. To get out of the bondage of debt and live a debt-free life, you must make a serious commitment, and then prepare a written plan. The basic elements of this plan are listed below:

1. Set a goal to get out of debt, and be determined to see it through. Once you have stopped deficit spending, you have taken a major step toward having victory over debt.

2. Determine how much money you owe. Get a total of your bills, and don't leave anything out. You need to know where you are financially. First, calculate your overall debt. Secondly, fill in the entire budget sheet (found at the end of chapter 9) to get an accurate account of your monthly expenses.

3. Prioritize your bills from the smallest to the largest. This is very important. Determine which bill has the smallest number of remaining payments.

4. Once you have identified the smallest bill, focus your attention on paying it first. You can give your action plan a boost by going through your home and identifying things you don't really need. Sell them, and apply the cash to that first bill.

5. After bill number one is paid, take the money that you were paying on bill number one, and apply it to bill number two. Then start paying on bill number two until it is paid in full. After bill number two is paid off, focus on bill number three until it is completely paid. Repeat this process until all your debts are paid.

Start a Savings Program

Fourthly, begin to save your money. If you spend less than you make, you will always have a surplus. You should set a goal to live on 70 percent of your income (see chapter 3 on planning). With a surplus account, you will be able to set aside a portion of your existing income for emergencies, to purchase things you really need, and to start an investment account for your family. This will be discussed further in chapter 8, which covers saving and investing. The main point is to start where you are with your existing income and to set aside something from every paycheck—even if it is only five to ten dollars per month. Set aside something.

Start Giving according to the Scriptures

Lastly, after you get your debts under control and start a savings program, implement your plans to immediately reach out to those around you—family, relatives, friends, neighbors, and coworkers. Once your debt is under control and you are living above your financial circumstances, you can help someone else learn how to get their personal finances under control. Here are some guidelines:

- $ Take a portion of all the money that you save on interest and give it to your local church (where you attend regularly).
- $ Give more than 10 percent (tithe) of your income to the Lord's work in your local church.
- $ Set up a reserve account specifically for giving to the poor and those who are in need.
- $ Identify ministries that have a proven record for missionary outreach and winning souls. Give liberally to these ministries. Remember that your money is an extension of you, and it can go places and work on your behalf.

BIBLICAL PRINCIPLES FOR ANY FINANCIAL DIFFICULTY

As you make an effort to become free from financial bondage, you should remember that there are principles outlined in the Bible that will bring you through any financial difficulty. There are five I have outlined so far in this book that will work if you will simply act on the principles themselves. These biblical principles are as follows:

1. Remember that God owns it all. As His steward, you should follow His instruction.
2. Spend less than you earn.
3. Have a plan of action.
4. Set something aside from each paycheck.
5. Avoid surety (long-term and inappropriate debt).

These principles are simple. For many of us, however, they will require drastic changes in our current lifestyles.

PRACTICAL APPLICATION

If you find yourself in over your head and want to start applying these principles to your life immediately, remember the following points:

$ Put God first. Plant a seed to God out of your firstfruits. "Honour the Lord with thy substance, and with the firstfruits of all thine increase" (Proverbs 3:9).

$ Pay yourself second. Whatever you give to God, you want to be in a position to set aside an equal amount for yourself (as a minimum). You must always have a surplus account (cash reserve), or you will be right back where you started when the first emergency occurs.

$ Reduce bills and outgoing expenses.

$ Use your budget, and live on a cash basis. If you don't have the cash, don't buy it.

$ Avoid any new debts.

CHAPTER 5

OPENING THE WINDOWS OF HEAVEN

*Honour the LORD with thy substance, and with the firstfruits of
all thine increase: so shall thy barns be filled with plenty, and
thy presses shall burst out with new wine.*
—Proverbs 3:9–10

*Give, and it will be given to you. A good measure, pressed down,
shaken together and running over, will be poured into your lap.
For with the measure you use, it will be measured to you.*
—Luke 6:38 NIV

I recall how my father managed his money when I was
growing up. He simply brought his paycheck home to my
mother, and she took care of all the bills. However, I remember one time when he cashed his check and treated some
friends to a night on the town. By the time he got home, nearly
all his money was gone!

Needless to say, my mother didn't think much of this approach to giving. Yet, this incident illustrates something about
the way my father looked at money. If it had been up to him, he
would have given it away. Spending the family's paycheck in
one evening on the town is certainly not an appropriate application of the principle of giving; however, my father had a very
generous heart, and throughout his life, he was blessed because
of it. He never met anyone he considered a stranger, and he
never turned down anybody who had a need or asked to borrow
money. He loved to help anyone who was in a financial bind or
had some kind of business venture. As far as I can remember, he
never knew he was following biblical principles, but he had a
giving heart.

I was the oldest of ten children, and I agreed with my mother. I never understood why my dad gave so much away. I wasn't aware of it at the time, but we were considered a poor family. Yet my father was always giving things away. What was it about my father that allowed him always to have something to give? I didn't realize until many years later that my father had learned how to tap into the principle of giving and receiving. As a result, he always had something to give, and it seemed he always had opportunities coming his way.

As I look back, I can see the results of my father's giving nature. He raised ten children and put four through college; and now, in his later years, he owns property in several locations—and it is all paid for. That is not a bad financial situation for a person who never finished the seventh grade.

Many individuals go through their lives without learning about sowing and reaping. One of the tragedies of our welfare system is that it restricts people from giving. It forces people to become takers, not givers, and then to turn totally inward. Welfare recipients become stagnant. The best way to get people off welfare is to teach them how to become valuable to someone else. They need to learn how to give of themselves first. The principle of giving and receiving will work for anyone who uses it. It will work for the Christian and non-Christian alike.

As Christians, we are supposed to have an impact for the kingdom of God. We are supposed to be God's agents for good on the earth. But all too often we spend all our time earning money just to pay bills. We don't have anything left to give.

GIVING AND RECEIVING

The purpose of this chapter is to deal with some areas of giving that are overlooked in many Christian circles. There are biblical guidelines for giving and receiving that every Christian should understand. Giving is God's way for us to tap into His supernatural blessings.

As we look around, we see this principle at work in the world. Think about the philanthropist who puts money into a foundation to be given away, even though the motivation may be to save on taxes. The more this person gives, the more blessings come his or her way. Or, consider a businessman who puts money into a new business venture with the expectation of receiving a return. The law of sowing and reaping will work for every person who uses it.

Sowing a seed is one of the most powerful principles outlined in the Bible in relation to our personal finances. However, perhaps it is also one of the most misunderstood. Every Christian should understand the benefit of giving to God with the right attitude:

> *But this I say, He which soweth sparingly shall reap also sparingly; and he which soweth bountifully shall reap also bountifully....And God is able to make all grace abound toward you; that ye, always having all sufficiency in all things, may abound* [give] *to every good work: (as it is written, He hath dispersed abroad; he hath given to the poor: his righteousness remaineth for ever).*
> (2 Corinthians 9:6, 8–9)

Two Sides of the Same Coin

Many Christians realize that they are supposed to give, but they are having problems in their personal finances because they don't fully understand the giving and receiving cycle. To fully understand giving, we must realize that giving and receiving are two sides of the same coin. To be able to give from one side, you must already have received on the other side. Of course, you can pledge a gift. However, according to the following Scripture, you can only give after you have received: *"For if the willingness is there, the gift is acceptable according to what one has, not according to what he does not have"* (2 Corinthians 8:12 NIV).

You can only give after you have received. According to the Scriptures, God gives seed to the sower so that a person will have something to give. *"Now he who supplies seed to the sower and bread for food will also supply and increase your store of seed and will enlarge the harvest of your righteousness"* (2 Corinthians 9:10 NIV). God always initiates the process. *"For God so loved the*

79

world, that he gave his only begotten Son, that whosoever believeth in him should not perish, but have everlasting life" (John 3:16). Notice that God loved us so much that He gave first. God gives to us, then He allows us the opportunity to give back out of what we have received. *"Upon the first day of the week let every one of you lay by him in store, as God hath prospered him"* (1 Corinthians 16:2).

RIGHT IN THE HEAD BUT WRONG IN THE HEART

I was counseling a Christian businessman in a city in which I was conducting a small-group financial study course. The businessman explained that his business had been successful; however, now he was having problems. He stated that when he had started to trust God, everything had begun to go wrong. "You can't run a business according to biblical guidelines and be successful. The two just don't mix," he said.

After examining his situation, I found that his problems had started after an evangelical meeting in which the minister had made the statement, "You can't outgive God." The businessman had gone to his cash register and had taken all the money and put it into the offering. He said he then began to "trust God to meet 100 percent of my needs."

In essence, you can't outgive God, but you must also use wisdom and common sense. There are other principles in the Bible that govern our finances besides just giving, and this businessman had broken most of them. One of these is honesty and integrity (see chapter 6). All the money in the register did not belong to the businessman to give! A portion of every dollar he had taken in had already been promised to others for the operating expenses of the business (suppliers, employees' salaries, utilities, etc.).

The problem was that the businessman had gotten just a part of the overall picture. He had to learn he was only a trustee of the money he had mismanaged. The same is true with our individual finances. If we as stewards don't set aside a portion of our incomes, we will be at the mercy of every emergency and problem that the Devil sends our way. Once we have promised to pay our utilities, credit cards, and other living expenses, we have made a commitment, and the money no longer belongs to us. We do not have the spiritual authority to give it away.

However, if we are obedient to God's Word, then we are in a position in which God can supernaturally meet our needs. There are times when God will lead us to make sacrificial gifts, as He led the widow who gave all the money she had (Mark 12:41–44) or the woman who shared her last meal with the prophet Elijah (1 Kings 17:10–16). Notice that God never asked them to break any biblical principle that He had given in the past.

Ignorance is no excuse with God. He wants our hearts and our actions to line up with His Word.

GIVING IN GRATITUDE TO GOD

Giving is a form of thanksgiving to God for what He has already given you. You have been blessed; now you have the opportunity to be a blessing to others. Once you have given, you have completed the giving and receiving cycle.

Receiving is as simple as giving. Many Christians are waiting for their "ship to come in." They say, "When I earn one hundred thousand dollars a year, I will give more to the Gospel," or, "When God blesses me with more money, I will give to the poor." The question is, What are you doing with what you have now? With most people, the future never comes. If you have a problem giving one hundred dollars, you will have more difficulty giving one thousand dollars.

You start where you are. By giving, the cycle is set. When you begin giving out of what you have, God will bless you with more to give in the future, because He will know you can be trusted.

GIVING IS A COMMITMENT YOU MAKE IN ADVANCE

I believe that in the last days, God will raise up individuals in the local church who can be trusted to give large sums of money to finance the Gospel. We know that God wants us to be in a position to give. Many Christians go through their entire lives with a desire to give, but they simply don't have the money. They have problems just meeting their own needs. How can they give to their local church or to the poor?

What is the problem? The answer is simple. Being in a position to give does not just happen; you must plan ahead today to be in a position to give in the future! Giving is not a feeling or an emotional outburst that happens suddenly. You must purpose in your heart (in advance) to be a giver.

In chapter 3, "Planning and Preparation," I suggested that you set aside 70 percent of your income for taxes and living expenses. The remaining 30 percent should be distributed among short-term and long-term savings and giving. One of your primary concerns should be giving. The purpose of this chapter is not to dictate the amount a person should give, but to emphasize that God should be at the top of your priority list.

God must be included in your planning. The tithe (10 percent) is the standard measuring stick for many Christians. Yet, I believe that 10 percent is only a beginning point for giving and that your giving should be led by the Holy Spirit. Remember that God owns it all, and that you are His steward. The more you can direct toward His kingdom, the better.

By using the biblical principles outlined in this book, you may be in a position to give 90 percent and live on 10 percent. If you are ever going to fulfill the desire God has put in your heart to be a giver, you must make a commitment to do it in advance.

GIVING IN ORDER TO GET

Another area of difficulty for many Christians is that of giving to receive something in return. Many Christians give money specifically to get more money from God. They believe that if they give a certain amount of money to certain causes, God is obligated to do something on their behalf just because they gave.

Let us look at this from a biblical perspective. It is not just indiscriminate giving that gets God's attention. You must give in faith according to biblical guidelines. The main reason some people receive more seed than others is that they have learned how to plug into the sowing and reaping principle. They know that if you plant a crop of soybeans, you will receive soybeans. The more you plant, the more you will receive. The better the ground and the better the cultivation, the greater the crop.

You should give in faith, expecting to receive a return based on God's Word:

> *But this I say, he which soweth sparingly shall reap also sparingly; and he which soweth bountifully shall reap also bountifully. Every man according as he purposeth in his heart, so let him give; not grudgingly, or of necessity: for God loveth a cheerful giver.* (2 Corinthians 9:6–7)

The Bible clearly points out that giving will cause material increase, but giving should also be a condition of the heart. *"And God is able to make all grace abound toward you; that ye, always having all sufficiency in all things, may abound to every good work"* (v. 8). The passage goes on to say that God will give seed to the sower:

> *Now he that ministereth seed to the sower both minister bread for your food, and multiply your seed sown, and increase the fruits of your righteousness; being enriched in every thing to all bountifulness, which causeth through us thanksgiving to God.* (2 Corinthians 9:10–11)

Nevertheless, we know that everyone does not have seed to sow. The question is, Who has the sower's heart? God will provide seed to those who are willing to sow.

THE SOWER'S HEART

Who has the sower's heart? If you were a businessman and were looking for someone to farm your land, which would you choose—a person who is a professional farmer or a person who believes he can be a good farmer? Who would more likely produce the best crop—the person who has been doing it for years with a proven track record or the person who says that he knows how to farm, but has no experience? The answer is obvious. The person with the proven track record would more likely produce the best crop. The experience he received from planting last year's crop gives him the knowledge to produce a better crop this year.

The same is true with our personal finances. The reason why some Christians don't have more seeds to plant is that they don't have a giving heart. They don't have experience in giving and a proven track record. They have not prepared themselves to be in a position to give.

We will discuss giving as a step of faith to receiving God's supernatural increase in more detail in chapter 12.

GIVING OURSELVES FIRST

To begin to implement the principle of giving, we need to start with giving ourselves to God: *"Present your bodies a living sacrifice, holy, acceptable unto God, which is your reasonable service"* (Romans 12:1).

The greatest gift mankind ever received was when God gave His only begotten Son Jesus Christ to the world. He gave because of His great love for us that is beyond anything we could ever comprehend. Because of the precious gift that God has given to us through His Son, we should also want to give to Him in return.

Our giving should come out of a personal relationship with Christ—a relationship of seeking His guidance and direction for our lives and having a daily walk with Him. We have a great responsibility as Christians to be sensitive to His Holy Spirit and to give as we are led.

Giving is an attitude of the heart. We should give cheerfully because we love the Lord and want to see His will done on the earth. We should also give in faith, with an expectancy that God will multiply our seed, as He has said in His Word. We need to make sure we understand that whenever God makes a promise in His Word, we are responsible to do our part to receive the promise. Based on this system, we know that God gives material blessings, but we must realize that there are other biblical principles that also have an impact on our personal finances. Remember that just because we give, God is not automatically obligated to intervene in our personal finances. If we are giving on the one hand and breaking other biblical principles governing economics on the other hand, then our finances will still be out of order.

HOW TO LAY UP TREASURES IN HEAVEN

Why should giving be one of our primary concerns, and why should we set aside some of our income to help those who are in need? These verses show that God has a special concern for the poor and needy:

Hearken, my beloved brethren, Hath not God chosen the poor of this world rich in faith, and heirs of the kingdom which he hath promised to them that love him?
(James 2:5)

He that hath mercy on the poor, happy is he.
(Proverbs 14:21)

He that hath pity upon the poor lendeth unto the LORD; and that which he hath given will he pay him again.
(Proverbs 19:17)

In these Scriptures, we see that when we give to the poor, we are lending to the Lord. The poor are not able to repay us, so God repays us. God cares about the needs of the poor, who are always with us. The Bible says, *"For ye have the poor always with you"* (Matthew 26:11). Yet, the Scriptures go on to say that it is our responsibility as Christians to help meet the needs of those who are less fortunate than we are. We are vessels for God to use to bless others in need.

Action Step

Set a goal of giving to the poor.

It is very important to realize the impact that giving to the poor has in laying a foundation in heaven. Jesus told a rich young ruler: *"One thing thou lackest: go thy way, sell whatsoever thou hast, and give to the poor, and thou shalt have treasure in heaven: and come, take up the cross, and follow me"* (Mark 10:21). We are storing up treasures in heaven when we give to the poor, as these verses reveal:

> *Charge them that are rich in this world, that they be not highminded, nor trust in uncertain riches, but in the living God, who giveth us richly all things to enjoy; that they do good, that they be rich in good works, ready to distribute, willing to communicate; laying up in store for themselves a good foundation against the time to come, that they may lay hold on eternal life.* (1 Timothy 6:17–19)

> *As it is written, He hath dispersed abroad; he hath given to the poor: his righteousness remaineth for ever.* (2 Corinthians 9:9)

> *Lay not up for yourselves treasures upon earth, where moth and rust doth corrupt, and where thieves break through and steal: but lay up for yourselves treasures in heaven, where neither moth nor rust doth corrupt, and where thieves do not break through nor steal.* (Matthew 6:19–20)

> *Sell what you have and give alms; provide yourselves money bags which do not grow old, a treasure in the heavens that does not fail, where no thief approaches nor moth destroys.* (Luke 12:33 NKJV)

GIVING WITH THE RIGHT ATTITUDE

People exhibit a variety of conflicting attitudes regarding giving. When I was growing up, I went to church every Sunday with my grandparents. Since my grandfather was the preacher, I had the opportunity to observe firsthand what happened when the offering plate was passed. Although my grandfather was a committed Christian, he never preached a sermon on giving. His focus was always on winning souls to Jesus. The offering was considered just a necessary part of the service; therefore, the attitude of most people was, "Let's get it over with as quickly as possible."

I watched the reaction of the congregation as the offering plate passed by. I noticed that several members were always late. They arrived just after the offering was over. Then there were the faithful, who would always put in a dollar and who usually would give a coin to their children so that they could give also. Next were those who looked as if they were being imposed upon when the offering plate came by; they usually gave nothing. Finally, there were others who felt obligated to put something in the plate.

As I look back, I see that my childhood experiences governed how I gave to the church when I became an adult. Since I had never had a biblical foundation for my giving, I formed my attitudes by what I saw others do.

As I talk to Christians today all over the country, I find that many of them grew up pretty much the same as I did. Some grew up in churches but never understood the importance of giving and receiving principles. Many Christians don't want to give because they don't understand what the Scriptures really say regarding giving. Once Christians who genuinely love the Lord learn what the Bible says about giving and receiving, their attitudes about giving change.

To summarize and to help you better understand the principles of giving and receiving, I have listed below some of the more common questions about giving that I encounter when teaching others how to put biblical stewardship into action.

PRACTICAL APPLICATION

Questions and Answers on Giving

Q. What is the main purpose of giving? Is it for our benefit or God's benefit? Explain.

A. Our benefit. God does not need our money. God uses giving as a means to bless us and to establish His covenant in the earth. The money never leaves the earth; only the things you do with the money go toward your heavenly account.

Q. What about sacrificial giving? Is it always right to give sacrificially?

A. Yes, sacrificial giving is very much a part of God's giving plan. It is for emergency situations and is discussed throughout the Bible. However, it is not always the best way to give, and it is not for every situation. God never intended for us to live from emergency to emergency.

Q. If I were to give to the poor, what part of my budget would the money come from?

A. The money would come from your surplus, not your tithes and obligations due other people. It should be set aside for this purpose.

Q. Is God obligated to perform a miracle in my finances just because I give or have a need? Why or why not?

A. No. You must be obedient to do what God's Word says. Your faith must be in operation. If you do your part, God will do His part.

Q. Can you plant a seed of something other than money and receive financial blessing? If so, explain.

A. Yes, you may plant a seed of whatever you have: time, love, friendship, abilities, talents, etc. Consider the passage in 1 Kings 17:8–16 about the woman who had a handful of meal and a little oil. She gave her last cake to the prophet and received a blessing that lasted until the drought was over. She gave (planted) the meal and oil, which was all she had, and she received a harvest through her obedience. (The same was true in the lives of Joseph and Daniel.)

Q. What is the principle of sowing and reaping that's involved when a businessman uses seed capital to start a new business?

A. He sows money into a business, and he reaps a harvest when the business becomes profitable.

Q. What about the principle of "gleaning"—how does it apply to seed time and harvest?

A. God provided a method in the Bible called gleaning, a means of giving to the poor out of the abundance God has given you. The guidelines for gleaning are presented in the Old

Testament. An example of this can be found in Ruth 2:2–23. You will find that, throughout the Bible, God makes special provisions for the poor. There is always a blessing for taking care of the poor. (Gleaning was not a part of the tithe.)

Q. Is God obligated to perform a miracle just because I am in a financial crisis?

A. No. If you stand on God's Word, trust in Him, and are obedient to what He says, He will deliver you. God operates according to His Word. If you obey His Word, God has obligated Himself to perform according to His Word.

Q. What about gimmicks used by preachers to entice you to give?

A. That is not an acceptable reason to give to God. You should be led by God's Spirit when giving to a ministry.

Q. What if you give and you find out that the minister didn't do what he said he would with the money?

A. If you gave in faith, with the right attitude as a steward, God will honor it. You are not giving to the minister, but to God. However, if you discover that a ministry is not honest, you should make every dollar count for the kingdom of God by switching your giving to ministries that have integrity.

Q. Should you give to bums and derelicts who ask for money?

A. It depends. If you feel led by God, do it. If you do not feel led by God, it is best not to give. You may want to give as an opportunity to witness to those in need.

CHAPTER 6

THE FOUNDATION OF ALL GOD'S BLESSINGS

The just man walketh in his integrity: his children
are blessed after him.
—Proverbs 20:7

A good name is rather to be chosen than great riches, and loving
favour rather than silver and gold.
—Proverbs 22:1

What is one of the most memorable events you can recall from your childhood? This was an essay question that a freshman college student had to answer for an English composition class. Her answer was a touching recollection that described the underlying strength of the character of her family.

She described an event that had stayed with her through the years. Her mother had gone to a restaurant's drive-through window. She had given the cashier a twenty dollar bill and taken the change in her hand. With the kids in the car, she had driven away without counting the money. She had almost gotten home when she noticed that the attendant had given her more change than she should have. It appeared that she had given her a ten dollar bill instead of a one dollar bill. They were halfway across town, but the mother turned the car around, went back to the restaurant, and told the attendant that she had given her too much change. "It is nice to meet an honest person these days," the grateful attendant said.

The young lady noticed that her mother never really said anything to her children, but that day they learned what real honesty was. Honesty is not a matter of money, but a condition of the heart. It is doing the right thing, even when it seems not to be in your best interest.

HONESTY AND INTEGRITY BRING BLESSINGS FROM GOD

Honesty and integrity will make you successful in God's financial system. They open the door for God to come into your financial circumstances, and they form the foundation for receiving His supernatural increase. All blessings from God, including financial blessings, come as a result of an honest heart. Honesty and integrity will definitely have an impact on your finances. Note their importance to our lives:

$ Wealth will be in the house of the honest and upright person: *"In the house of the righteous is much treasure: but in the revenues of the wicked is trouble"* (Proverbs 15:6).

$ Your children will be blessed: *"The just man walketh in his integrity: his children are blessed after him"* (Proverbs 20:7).

$ Even if you make mistakes, God will lift you up: *"For a just man falleth seven times, and riseth up again: but the wicked shall fall into mischief"* (Proverbs 24:16).

$ An honest person is valuable to others: *"The tongue of the just is as choice silver: the heart of the wicked is little worth"* (Proverbs 10:20).

$ Honesty will keep you out of trouble: *"The wicked is snared by the transgression of his lips: but the just shall come out of trouble"* (Proverbs 12:13).

$ A good name and an honest reputation are more valuable than great riches: *"A good name is rather to be chosen than great riches, and loving favour rather than silver and gold"* (Proverbs 22:1).

$ A truthful person is a delight to God: *"Lying lips are abomination to the LORD: but they that deal truly are his delight"* (Proverbs 12:22).

$ Honesty is obedience to God: *"Ye shall not steal, neither deal falsely, neither lie one to another"* (Leviticus 19:11).

$ If you are honest, God will guide you: *"The integrity of the upright shall guide them: but the perverseness of transgressors shall destroy them"* (Proverbs 11:3).

$ God will not withhold any good thing from those who are honest and upright: *"For the LORD God is a sun and shield: the LORD will give grace and glory: no good thing will he withhold from them that walk uprightly"* (Psalm 84:11).

$ Honesty and integrity will preserve you: *"Let integrity and uprightness preserve me; for I wait on thee"* (Psalm 25:21).

$ God will be merciful and bless those who walk in integrity: *"But as for me* [David], *I will walk in mine integrity: redeem me, and be merciful unto me"* (Psalm 26:11).

$ Honesty and wisdom go together: *"Better is the poor that walketh in his integrity, than he that is perverse in his lips, and is a fool"* (Proverbs 19:1).

$ God will be intimate with the honest person: *"For the perverse person is an abomination to the LORD, but His secret counsel is with the upright"* (Proverbs 3:32 NKJV).

$ An honest person will be established forever: *"The lip of truth shall be established for ever: but a lying tongue is but for a moment"* (Proverbs 12:19).

$ An honest man will not take bribes and will keep trouble out of his house: *"He who is greedy for gain troubles his own house, but he who hates bribes will live"* (Proverbs 15:27 NKJV).

$ An honest person will not lie to become rich: *"The getting of treasures by a lying tongue is a vanity tossed to and fro of them that seek death"* (Proverbs 21:6).

God is looking for individuals who have honesty and integrity of heart to trust with the true riches.

CAN YOU BE TRUSTED?

A class I taught was discussing the day's homework assignments, when Janet, one of the students, made a comment. She explained that her son worked as a local supermarket cashier. He had come home one day and told her about something that had happened. He had gone to the bank to cash his check. He discovered after he returned to work that the bank teller had accidentally put one hundred dollars too much in his envelope. His coworkers told him that since it was the teller's mistake, he should keep the money. However, he went to his supervisor and told him what had happened and asked if he would let him off work for a half hour so he could return the money.

As their instructor, I told the group, "Janet's story is a good example of honesty and integrity."

Janet quickly added, "That's not the whole story." She went on to explain that about four months later, her son's cash register came up short of money. Her son indicated that he had done nothing wrong, but he could not explain how the money had disappeared from his register.

Normally, the cashier would have been fired immediately, but the supervisor was not convinced that Janet's son had taken the money because of the earlier incident with the one hundred dollars. They learned that someone had used him and set a trap without his knowledge. Another individual had been using the number to his register to get access to it without anyone knowing. The main reason the son didn't get fired was because his manager did not believe that a thief would have returned one hundred dollars to a bank when the bank had made a mistake. This story illustrates the value of having a good reputation.

According to the Bible, it is true that God has promised to bless us financially. But it is also true that God allows financial blessings to be taken away from those who don't have integrity of heart or those who don't know how to properly handle the money with which they have been entrusted.

Take therefore the talent [money] from him, and give it unto him which hath ten talents. For unto every one that hath shall be given, and he shall have abundance: but from him that hath not shall be taken away even that which he hath. (Matthew 25:28–29)

For riches certainly make themselves wings; they fly away as an eagle toward heaven. (Proverbs 23:5)

Wealth gotten by vanity shall be diminished: but he that gathereth by labour shall increase. (Proverbs 13:11)

HOW GOOD IS YOUR WORD?

Can you really be trusted to keep your word? Do your words say one thing, but your actions say something different? Are you honest in everything that you do? Christians must walk in honesty and integrity—before God and before man. Living in our times, in this society, we are all confronted every day with matters of honesty and integrity. When we go to the cafeteria, are we tempted to try to avoid paying for items that we have received? At the grocery store, when we go through the checkout line, if we receive more money in change than we should, do we return it? On our taxes, do we overstate certain deductions? Concerning insurance, do we add more to our claims than should really be there in order to receive greater benefits than we deserve?

Action Step

Walk in total honesty with God
and man.

DO YOU REALLY TRUST GOD AT HIS WORD?

If we believe, in fact, that God's Word is truth, we must act on it. This is the basic definition of faith. God promised in His Word that He'll take care of us, that He'll meet our needs if we'll accept the promises that He has given us. Then we can walk in certainty and believe that God will perform the promises that He has made. Dishonesty and lying indicate that we do not have complete trust in God's Word to provide what He indicated He would provide for us in our lives. *"He that walketh in his uprightness feareth the* LORD: *but he that is perverse in his ways despiseth him"* (Proverbs 14:2). Being honest with God is having confidence in His Word—believing that His Word is true.

Action Step

Have confidence that God will
perform His promises.

Most instances of dishonesty come about when a person cares more about his or her own desires than the desires of another person. Most of the problems that we have in today's society come as a result of someone wanting to take advantage of property that someone else owns.

Action Step

Avoid personal and business
associations with dishonest people.

Because of advertising and our materialistic society, we've been taught to covet things that belong to others. We've been "programmed" to want bigger homes and larger cars. From television and other secular entertainment, we are taught to covet even our neighbors' wives or husbands. The basic idea is to look out for number one. This is the system that operates in the world. But God has another system, and it operates on a completely different set of principles and guidelines. *"Thou shalt love thy neighbour as thyself"* (Romans 13:9).

God wants you to be honest in dealing with your business and work affairs. Even the smallest dishonesty displeases God and is a sin. An important part of the stewardship principle in the Bible is reflected in this verse: *"Whoever is dishonest with very little will also be dishonest with much"* (Luke 16:10 NIV).

> ### Action Step
>
> Do an honest day's work for an
> honest day's pay.

Do you feel you have to tell a little white lie to protect yourself and your property? In work and business, are you honest with your employer? Are you honest with your employees? As a worker, God wants you to be an example to the people who work around you. Do you provide an honest day's work for an honest day's pay? Do you carry yourself in a way that projects honesty in everything you do?

Do you check in to work on time, or do you take a few minutes too long on your coffee breaks? Do you take things home from work that don't belong to you? God's requirement is that we be honest first before Him and then before our neighbors and the people around us.

> ### Action Step
>
> Always be honest with friends and
> coworkers. If you are in a position
> of authority, be honest with your
> employees and look out for their
> interests.

TELLTALE SIGNS OF A DISHONEST HEART

Because of the decrease in society's standards, many people, even Christians, are dishonest without ever realizing it. Can you be trusted with money? Do you have a bad credit report? Do you pay your bills on time? How we conduct ourselves will have an impact on people around us. Likewise, we are influenced by the people with whom we work and associate. A good name and reputation should be maintained at all times. Keep your word, pay your bills on time, and don't make commitments that you can't keep:

A good name is rather to be chosen than great riches, and loving favour rather than silver and gold. (Proverbs 22:1)

When a man makes a vow [promise] to the LORD or takes an oath to obligate himself by a pledge [commits himself], he must not break his word but must do everything he said. (Numbers 30:2 NIV)

Action Step

Maintain a good reputation and
pay your bills on time.

Bankruptcy is not an option as far as a Christian is concerned. Certainly, a Christian can get into a difficult situation regarding debt. But a Christian should not intentionally go in and purchase things with the thought that he or she can get out of paying for them by filing for bankruptcy.

Action Step

Never voluntarily file for bankruptcy
because of your debt.

How is your credit report? You should always maintain a good credit rating. Check your credit file, and see if it has accurate information. Many times the credit reporting agency has outdated or inaccurate data. As good stewards, children of God must be beyond reproach as they conduct business affairs before the unsaved world. Everything we do is under scrutiny and is a testimony to someone else, whether we realize it or not. This is especially true regarding how we pay our bills and handle personal obligations.

There's no better way to judge a person's character than to watch how he or she handles money during hard times. God wants us to be good witnesses and to have a good testimony in the world. He wants our words to be consistent with our actions. Our names should be synonymous with character and integrity.

Recall that if we are not diligent with unrighteous money, we won't be diligent with the true riches. When we make vows, we must keep them. If we promise to pay our bills on a certain date, we must pay them on that date even if we have to make personal sacrifices to do it.

Action Step

Always maintain a good credit report. Check your credit report annually to make sure it is accurate.

If we are to be good stewards, we must be people who keep our word. As I wrote earlier, Joshua made a promise to certain tribes. Even though he was deceived, he had to keep his promise. (See Joshua 9.) A price had to be paid simply because Joshua had made a promise, even though he had not had all of the facts. The Scripture states that it is better not to make a vow than to make a vow and not keep it (Deuteronomy 23:21–22). We must keep the vows, commitments, and promises that we have made. We must walk honestly before God and man.

Action Step

Always keep your word, and do not make promises you cannot keep.

God is looking for people He can trust to be coworkers with Him in establishing His covenant in the earth. We must remember that every one of our actions is a testimony to someone around us. What we say, what we do, and how we conduct our business are all being closely watched by those who do not know Christ to see if what we claim about Him is working in our lives. Your name is a combination of the words you speak and the actions you take. Your name is worth more than money.

In short, our lives should be a living testimony to both Christians and the unsaved—at work, at home, and in the eyes of the general public—that God's way of doing business is not only different from the world's way of doing business, but that God's way is also better.

PRACTICAL APPLICATION

Read the following questions regarding honesty and integrity. If you feel that you are involved in any of these activities or other activities that you feel are not pleasing to God, ask God to forgive you. Then make a specific effort to correct these areas. Set personal goals to eliminate any of the items that you feel that God is bringing to your attention.

- $ Am I on time or am I constantly late for appointments?
- $ Do I report all taxable income and all my expenses legitimately? Do I have bounced checks on my personal checking account?
- $ Do I keep my promises to my children?
- $ Do I provide an honest day's work for an honest day's pay?
- $ Have I made a vow (pledge) to give something to God or man but not kept my promise because I felt I needed it more? Do I spend more money than I earn?
- $ Do I care for others' property as well as I do for my own—for example, my employer's property or property that I borrow or use that belongs to someone else?
- $ Do I have a habit of telling only partial truths or stretching the truth or telling little white lies?
- $ Do I find myself avoiding friends and relatives because I owe them money?
- $ Do I ever misappropriate office supplies, stamps, or anything else of my employer's?
- $ If I am undercharged for a purchase in a checkout line, do I keep the money or report it?
- $ When dealing with other people, do I look out for their interests as well as my own?

$ Do I have bad credit? Am I honest in meeting my obligations and keeping commitments that I've made?

$ When I sell a car, house, or other property, do I tell the whole story or do I keep something back that I should reveal in order to get a larger profit?

CHAPTER 7

RELEASING OPPORTUNITY IN YOUR LIFE

He becometh poor that dealeth with a slack hand:
but the hand of the diligent maketh rich.
—Proverbs 10:4

Be thou diligent to know the state of thy flocks,
and look well to thy herds.
—Proverbs 27:23

I was sitting across the desk from Pat, who had attended one of my financial study courses. "My husband and I had something very interesting happen to us last week," she said.

"Okay, what was that?" I asked.

"Mel just got an increase in pay at his job," Pat continued.

"That's good news," I said. "Tell me what happened."

"Well, do you remember that at one of your workshops, you said that we should try to make ourselves valuable to our employers?"

"Yes, I remember that."

"Well, Mel thought about that, and at work he noticed that the grass around the edge of the parking lot needed to be cut. He figured that because he didn't have a college degree, he would not be able to do some of the other things at the warehouse. So he took it upon himself to tackle this particular chore. Without being asked, he started to cut the grass and keep the lawn clean with no request for pay.

"He continued this for a while without any special recognition for his efforts. Well, last week one of the marketing employees moved on to another job. The owner of the business asked Mel if he would like to have that job, which has the potential for much greater increases in pay. But, he also asked Mel if he would like to take over the maintenance contract on the building, which will amount to an additional three to four hundred dollars per month above the salary he will be paid for the new job."

God rewards diligence, and God will reward the work of your hands—if you do your work as if you were doing it for God, not man:

> *And whatsoever ye do, do it heartily, as to the Lord, and not unto men; knowing that of the Lord ye shall receive the reward of the inheritance: for ye serve the Lord Christ.*
> (Colossians 3:23–24)

DILIGENCE BRINGS PROSPERITY

In this chapter, we will explore the benefits of diligence, which is another biblical principle that prepares us for God's supernatural increase. Work is the pathway out of poverty. Diligence and hard work will change your financial circumstances. If you work, you will be rewarded. Diligence and work go hand in hand.

All work is honorable. Work provides an income stream that gives you and God something on which to build. Examine the following Scriptures:

> *Let him that stole steal no more: but rather let him labour, working with his hands the thing which is good, that he may have to give to him that needeth.* (Ephesians 4:28)

> *For even when we were with you, this we commanded you, that if any would not work, neither should he eat.*
> (2 Thessalonians 3:10)

> *He becometh poor that dealeth with a slack hand: but the hand of the diligent maketh rich.* (Proverbs 10:4)

> *The hand of the diligent shall bear rule: but the slothful shall be under tribute.* (Proverbs 12:24)

BE INDUSTRIOUS IN BUSINESS AFFAIRS

If you work, you can build wealth, if you manage your money properly. Even if you are an average wage earner with a relatively small income, God can supernaturally bless your income if you are obedient and follow His Word.

> *Seest thou a man diligent in his business? he shall stand before kings; he shall not stand before mean* [obscure] *men.* (Proverbs 22:29)

> *Be thou diligent to know the state of thy flocks, and look well to thy herds. For riches are not for ever: and doth the crown endure to every generation?* (Proverbs 27:23–24)

If your household earns twenty-five thousand dollars a year, that's over one million dollars during a lifetime. Once you realize that it is God who blesses you with money so that you can be a good steward, you must be diligent to manage it properly.

HOW TO PROSPER DURING HARD ECONOMIC TIMES

Pat and Mel's story at the beginning of this chapter reminds me of another situation, which concerned Sissy, with whom I worked at an investment company. She was in sales and marketing, but she wasn't doing well as a salesperson. At the time, her sales volume was low compared to the other sales staff. She was a diligent worker and tried hard to increase her sales but had no immediate success.

"We need someone to learn how to monitor the mutual fund activities," was a constant complaint from a number of more successful marketing people.

Since no other salesperson would take the responsibility because they felt it was a distraction, Sissy volunteered. "I'll organize and file the mutual fund material," she said. She took on the added responsibility right away. After organizing the files, she began to keep track of each mutual fund's performance and took it upon herself to order each company's brochure to keep on file. Not only did she keep up with the major companies, but she also assisted other salespeople in filing initial applications.

She became known as the in-house mutual fund expert. Yet many of the salespeople ridiculed her for doing extra services without additional pay.

Everything was going well in the investment business until the stock market "crash" of October 1987. Shortly thereafter, many investment companies found themselves in trouble because of the change in the economy. The investment company for which Sissy worked had to cut back on staff by 50 percent. I saw Sissy at a restaurant sometime later and asked her how she was doing.

"Dwight, I'm doing great. You know, the company had to cut back, and they let half of the people go, but they kept me because they needed someone to handle mutual fund business. Also, my sales volume has picked up."

"Yes? That's great, but tell me about your sales increase," I said.

"Well, after all the big-time salespeople dropped out of the business, the company gave me a chance to service some of the old accounts. Now my business is triple what it used to be."

God will always bless diligence and hard work!

Action Step

Make yourself valuable to your employer. Look for additional ways to help your employer become more successful.

HOW TO KEEP YOUR JOB DURING LAYOFFS

What about following the examples of Mel and Sissy and making yourself valuable to your employer? Many things can be done. *"And whosoever shall compel thee to go a mile, go with him twain* [two]*"* (Matthew 5:41).

You can make yourself valuable by learning what your company is all about, then retraining yourself to assist your company to make more money or to help your employer save money in existing areas. Your responsibility as an employee is to make your supervisor look good, to make your organization look good.

Here are some ways to make yourself indispensable:

1. Become familiar with your company's overall business. Learn what it takes to make a profit, and become valuable in the process.

2. Learn your job and the jobs of those around you. Assist others in their jobs.

3. Learn how to plant seeds. Take on responsibilities without having to be told to do so.

4. Be the first to help out when there is something extra that needs to be done.

5. Become dependable and trustworthy.

Because of your hard work and willingness to go the extra mile for your company, you will be rewarded not only by your boss, but by God as well.

These principles are almost absent from the average workplace. They have been replaced by this attitude: "I'll work if you pay me first. I'll do only the work that is required of me. I'll come in late and leave early. If I can get by with it, I'll do as little as possible on the job."

Action Step

Do your work as if you were doing it for the Lord, and God will reward you.

Many of us spend one-third of our lives working, laying down a third of our lives to earn a paycheck. Therefore, it is important for us as Christians to balance our lives and learn how to submit our work as a gift to God. God must have more than equal time; He must be in first place.

Action Step

Dedicate your work to the Lord and
use it as part of your worship.

HOW LONG SHOULD WE WORK?

God established the general parameters for the amount of
time we should spend working each week: *"Six days thou shalt
work, but on the seventh day thou shalt rest: in earing time and
in harvest thou shalt rest"* (Exodus 34:21).

There is a wide variation in working schedules in our society, but the most common is the eight-hour day, five-day week.
The most important factor that we should recognize in answering the question of how much we should work is that we should
work hard, but not overwork. The current trend is to lean toward either of two extremes. The one extreme is not to work at
all and to depend on someone else or the government to furnish
your needs. The other extreme is to become so involved in your
work that you tend to overextend yourself and neglect God, your
family, and your health.

A good way to keep work in balance is to remember your
major priorities, which were discussed earlier in this book. Your
first priority is God. *"But seek ye first the kingdom of God, and
his righteousness; and all these things shall be added unto you"*
(Matthew 6:33). Your second priority is your family, and your
third priority is your profession. If you are neglecting God or
your family by working, you are overworking.

THE RESPONSIBILITY OF THE EMPLOYEE

An employee's responsibility is to be faithful to his or her
employer. If you are an employee, remember that you have been
hired to do a job so that your employer can make a profit. You
must produce more than the expenses necessary to pay your
salary to be productive to your employer. *"And whatsoever ye
do, do it heartily, as to the Lord, and not unto men; knowing that*

of the Lord ye shall receive the reward of the inheritance: for ye serve the Lord Christ" (Colossians 3:23–24).

If you take a job for a low salary, you should do your work just as if your employer were paying you double. God will move heaven and earth to reward you, even if your employer or supervisor doesn't recognize your work, and you will be blessed. The blessing may come from a source other than your employer, but God will always find a way to bless a person who is diligent in work and who works in faith as unto the Lord.

Many employees forget their responsibilities after they are hired. You should always do excellent work, regardless of how you feel about your job or your employer. If you are doing your work as unto the Lord, your work will be of a quality second to none.

> *Servants, be obedient to them that are your masters according to the flesh, with fear and trembling, in singleness of your heart, as unto Christ; not with eyeservice, as menpleasers; but as the servants of Christ, doing the will of God from the heart; with good will doing service, as to the Lord, and not to men: knowing that whatsoever good thing any man doeth, the same shall he receive of the Lord, whether he be bond or free.* (Ephesians 6:5–8)

THE RESPONSIBILITY OF THE EMPLOYER

An employer is responsible for being honest and fair with employees. An employer must look out for the interests of his or her employees as well as his or her own interests: *"Masters, give unto your servants that which is just and equal; knowing that ye also have a Master in heaven"* (Colossians 4:1).

In the world's economy, the biblical principles of justness and fairness to employees are not often followed. Many employers are not sensitive to the needs of their employees. Their intention is to push their employees as far as possible to do a maximum amount of work. As a result of this kind of mindset, labor unions were formed to protect the rights of the employee. If the biblical principle of treating employees honestly and fairly had been acknowledged by employers, it never would have been necessary for labor unions to develop.

An employer should pay employees a fair and reasonable wage. Once an employee has performed his or her responsibilities, the worker should be paid on time. *"Thou shalt not defraud thy neighbour, neither rob him: the wages of him that is hired shall not abide with thee all night until the morning"* (Leviticus 19:13).

FINISH WHAT YOU START

Whenever you take on a job, do it well. You should always make a habit of completing your work. Many of us make promises and take on responsibilities without counting the cost. Many of our lives are a series of unfinished projects. We are busy doing many things, but we leave much undone. Whenever God started something, He completed it, and He wants us to do the same. Remember, whenever you do a job, you should do it as if you are doing it for God and not for man.

In conclusion, there are two things we should remember. First, God ordained work in the beginning. He created it for our benefit. *"And the LORD God took the man, and put him into the garden of Eden to dress it and to keep it"* (Genesis 2:15). This took place before the Fall. Many individuals believe that work came as a result of Adam's sin and that work is part of the Curse. But this Scripture lets us know that God never intended man to sit idly by and do nothing. He instituted work in the Garden of Eden when man was created. The Curse came later. (See Genesis 3:17–19.)

We work to earn money so that we can provide the essentials for our families to live. Paul stated, *"If any would not work, neither should he eat"* (2 Thessalonians 3:10). We also work so that we may have enough money to give to others and to extend a helping hand to them. *"Let him that stole steal no more: but rather let him labour, working with his hands the thing which is good, that he may have to give to him that needeth"* (Ephesians 4:28). Work definitely has an impact on personal finances. It is an essential key to building a sound financial foundation.

Secondly, we should be diligent in everything to which we set our hands. We need to do our work as if we were working for the Lord Himself. *"And whatsoever ye do, do it heartily, as to the Lord, and not unto men; knowing that oτ the Lord ye shall receive the reward oτ the inheritance: τor ye serve the Lord Christ"* (Colossians 3:23–24). We should remember that God, not our employer, is our provider.

PRACTICAL APPLICATION

Regarding the practical side of work, remember that when God gives you something, it will not put you into bondage. Consequently, there are five common mistakes related to work that should be avoided:

- $ Never make your spouse work just to improve your lifestyle unless you are both in agreement and know you are fulfilling God's purpose in your lives.
- $ God's wealth comes through diligence and discipline. It is not dependent upon the amount of money you earn.
- $ Make every dollar count. Look for ways to eliminate waste, and buy things wholesale. Pay cash when it is in your favor to do so.
- $ Set a goal to spend less money than you earn so that you will have a surplus account.
- $ Avoid quitting one job until you already have another or an alternative source of income lined up.

Be sure to remember that God is the provider of supernatural increase. If you are following biblical guidelines in managing your finances, you will see an increase. Be patient, and God will always be faithful to His Word.

CHAPTER 8

CHANGING SURPLUS INTO ABUNDANCE

*Steady plodding brings prosperity; hasty speculation
brings poverty.*
—Proverbs 21:5 TLB

*The wise man saves for the future, but the foolish man spends
whatever he gets.*
—Proverbs 21:20 TLB

I was driving down the highway with my radio tuned to the news channel. Suddenly, the national news headline was announced: "Custodial Worker Beats Wall Street." That immediately got my attention. I thought this was a strange opening for a national news update.

I listened anxiously for the follow-up story: "Custodial worker in Detroit leaves seven hundred thousand dollars to a Catholic girls' home." I wondered what was so spectacular about this incident. The custodial worker had died, and the money had been delivered to the girls' home. Another three hundred eighty thousand dollars was found in a mutual fund account owned by the custodian.

No one could figure out how a person seventy years of age, with a menial job, could have accumulated such a substantial sum of money. This was an unusual story. However, I was expecting the announcer to come back with a statement such as, "Custodial worker puts a few thousand dollars on stock option and wins a fortune." This would have been more spectacular.

Even though I thought this was an interesting story, I wondered why it would occupy a major part of the national newscast. Then it occurred to me that this was indeed a newsworthy story. The average American will never accumulate any real wealth because most people spend everything they earn. They don't understand the value of compound interest. Many do not understand even the basic principles of saving and investing.

SAVINGS AND INVESTMENTS

A small surplus over time becomes abundance with the proper use of compound interest. This is a key principle that governs God's financial system and it should be understood by every Christian. The next three chapters will focus on showing you how to build wealth God's way by eliminating waste and properly redirecting the resources you already have. They will examine how money actually works, how to turn surplus into abundance, how to start where you are, and how to use what you have as a steward over God's resources. As Christians, we should maximize every dollar that God has entrusted to our care.

Many of the principles discussed in the next two chapters will be elementary to some, but life-changing and exciting to others. Keep in mind that this information can function only as a guideline and is not intended to be used as a specific recommendation. Use it as a helpful aid for organizing your financial plan according to the goal that God has laid on your heart. It is best to consult sound financial advisors when making important decisions regarding your finances. The Scriptures say, *"Where there is no counsel, the people fall; but in the multitude of counselors there is safety"* (Proverbs 11:14 NKJV). Some people wait until they have a large estate before they do financial planning. However, it is always best to plan ahead so that you can make wise decisions about building and maintaining your financial base.

DEVELOPING YOUR SURPLUS

Developing a surplus has already been discussed in some detail (see chapter 3). If you spend less money than you take in, you will always have a surplus. Your first goal, then, in becoming free from financial bondage, is to learn how to develop excess funds.

Satan understands that if he can't keep you from developing a surplus, he can't limit the amount of money you have to invest into the kingdom of God. When you develop a surplus, you move past just getting your personal needs met to being able to reach out to others.

You are a steward of God's financial resources, and He wants you to know that His abundance is already built into His economic system. However, you must use your faith and be obedient to God's Word in order to be a channel that God can use.

> *For unto every one that hath shall be given, and he shall have abundance: but from him that hath not shall be taken away even that which he hath.* (Matthew 25:29)

> *For ye know the grace of our Lord Jesus Christ, that, though he was rich, yet for your sakes he became poor, that ye through his poverty might be rich.* (2 Corinthians 8:9)

> *For I mean not that other men be eased, and ye burdened: but by an equality, that now at this time your abundance may be a supply for their want, that their abundance also may be a supply for your want: that there may be equality.* (2 Corinthians 8:13–14)

After you develop a surplus, you must find a place to store it. Remember from the third chapter that God wants you to be a good steward over the whole dollar, not just part of it. What do you do with the other 90 percent after you give 10 percent to God? Again, you first set a goal to live on 70 percent of your income instead of spending everything you earn. After giving a minimum of 10 percent to your local church, this will leave you with a surplus of 20 percent (see figure 4).

FIGURE 4
Outgoing Expenditures
Your Budgetary Dollar

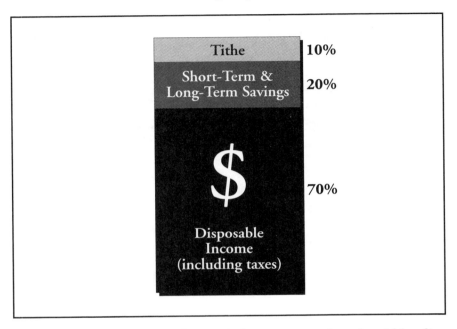

The 20 percent that figure 4 shows as surplus should be distributed between your short-term and long-term savings accounts. In order to organize this surplus, there are a number of basic strategies that the average Christian can use that are key to eliminating waste and developing a sound financial plan. These strategies will be used as the basis for most of the action steps for financial freedom discussed in the next three chapters.

WHAT BANKS AND INVESTMENT COMPANIES DON'T TELL YOU

This section provides answers to important investment questions that many people are asking themselves, yet are unsure where to find the information.

To begin with, you should take control of your personal financial affairs and never blindly leave them to someone else to handle. The reason why banks and financial institutions are the wealthiest businesses in the country is that they look out for their interests first. The system is designed to work in their favor. Your interests are a secondary factor.

The following is crucial information that you won't normally learn from your bankers or investment advisors:

1. Banks, insurance companies, and investment bankers don't tell you how your money works. For example, they don't usually tell you that a small surplus over time becomes an abundance with the proper use of compound interest.

2. If you spend less money than you earn, you will always have a surplus for investments.

3. You can be your own banker and invest your money at the same rate that the insurance companies and banks do (cutting out the middleman).

4. Compound interest will make you wealthy if you allow it to work for you instead of for your bank or investment company.

5. Fees and commissions will rob you of valuable investment resources and interest income.

6. Time and consistency work in your favor. When you set aside a little bit each month, it will become a large amount over time.

7. You can start where you are, using what you already have, and begin your investment program by eliminating expensive fees and commissions.

Action Step

Avoid paying unnecessary fees and commissions.

LEARN HOW BANKS AND INVESTMENT COMPANIES WORK

You should learn how banks, insurance companies, and investment companies actually work. An insurance company makes money from the premium you pay each month, and it profits from investing the surplus funds. Salespeople make a commission every time you buy a policy.

An investment company makes money from commissions, fees, and the interest it makes on the money it has invested. Whenever you buy or sell an investment, you pay your broker a transaction fee and/or a commission. The broker makes money on each transaction regardless of the financial results you receive.

Banks operate on the same principle. They make money on the difference between what they pay you in interest on your savings and what they receive by investing your money. They also charge fees for transactions you make at the bank.

It is important for you to know that each of these institutions operates by encouraging you to bring your money to them so that they can invest it for you. In most cases, you can make the same investments for yourself and put the income from the investments in your pocket instead of the institution's.

In most investment companies, the cards are stacked against the average investor. Most of the time the broker will be tempted to sell you the product that pays him or her the highest commission. However, you can invest in a no-load mutual fund, which means that you do not pay a commission up front when you open your investment account. This fact is important because your entire investment goes to work for you immediately. By identifying no-load or low-load mutual funds, the average family can avoid paying excessive commissions and fees on their investment transactions.

HOW TO CHOOSE THE RIGHT NO-LOAD MUTUAL FUND

Choosing the right mutual fund family is easy once you know what your objectives are. The following is a step-by-step guide to help you in this process.

1. Consult financial magazines. Each year they have a list of the top-performing mutual fund families. You can contact these mutual fund companies directly and ask for a prospectus.

2. Select a family of funds that handles a stock fund, bond fund, and money market fund—and has telephone switching capabilities.

3. Select a mutual fund that requires a minimum initial deposit within your investing limits.

4. By using the money movement strategy discussed in this chapter, select the correct type of mutual fund for the existing economy.

5. Select a fund that has assets of more than twenty-five million and less than two billion dollars.

6. Do not select a mutual fund on its five-year or ten-year total performance. Rather, select one based on its track record for the kind of economy in which you intend to use it.

Or, if you choose to work with a broker on the implementation of your long-term investment plan, he or she will normally have all the above information on file. Before you invest, simply ask your broker to send you a copy of the prospectus for the fund you are considering.

BUILD A MILLION DOLLAR RETIREMENT ACCOUNT

This section will show you the great benefits of having compound interest work for you instead of against you. You can use payroll deductions to start an IRA (individual retirement account). By investing a small amount of money over a period of time, even a modest investment can grow into a substantial retirement account. The key is time and consistency.

> **Action Step**
>
> Learn how compound interest works.

Consider the following example. If you invested one thousand dollars per year (about $2.74 per day) at 9 percent interest at the age of twenty-five, you would have thirty-two thousand dollars at the age of sixty-five (with compound interest). By using the "Rule of Seventy-Two," you can determine how many years it would take for your money to double. The Rule of Seventy-Two is a guideline for estimating how long it will take an investment to double in value. In this particular example, by dividing seventy-two by nine (the interest rate), you find that it would take approximately eight years for your money to double (see table 1, below).

Action Step

Use the Rule of 72 to determine how long it would take your money to double at a given interest rate.

TABLE 1

Investing $1,000 at 9 Percent Interest *

Age	Amount
25	$1,000
33	$2,000
41	$4,000
49	$8,000
57	$16,000
65	$32,000

* If you start with a one-thousand-dollar investment at age twenty-five and receive 9 percent interest until age sixty-five. These are only approximate figures that may vary with electronic calculation. The "Rule of Seventy-Two," which was used to determine these figures, is a guideline for estimating how long it will take an investment to double in value.

From table 1, you can see the effect of compound interest. Again, if you start with only a one-thousand-dollar investment at age twenty-five, it will grow to thirty-two thousand dollars by the time you are sixty-five, at the indicated interest rate.

To illustrate the point of what it means to be a wise and skillful investor, consider the following: If you would receive thirty-two thousand dollars on a one-hundred-dollar investment at 9 percent, how much would you receive at retirement if the interest rate were 18 percent (about the average interest rate on major credit cards)? Before you consult the next table, make a quick estimate of what you feel this amount would be. Then look at table 2 to check your answer.

TABLE 2

Investing $1,000 at 18 Percent Interest *

Age	Amount
25	$1,000
29	$2,000
33	$4,000
37	$8,000
41	$16,000
45	$32,000
49	$64,000
53	$128,000
57	$256,000
61	$512,000
65	$1,024,000

*If you start with a one-thousand-dollar investment, using compound interest. These are only approximate figures that may vary with electronic calculation.

STEADY PLODDING

Steady plodding brings prosperity; hasty speculation brings poverty. (Proverbs 21:5 TLB)

If a person were to invest one dollar a day at 12 percent interest from age twenty-five until he or she retired at age sixty-five, this person would accumulate more than three hundred thousand dollars at retirement. This is less than the cost of one pack of cigarettes or a couple of trips to the soft drink machine. At 12 percent interest on the three-hundred-thousand-dollar principal, this person would earn approximately thirty-six thousand dollars per year in interest payments without touching the principal.

If a person were to save $2.74 a day (approximately one thousand dollars per year) at 12.5 percent interest starting at the age of twenty-five, the person would receive over $1.1 million dollars when he or she reached retirement at age 65. At 12.5 percent interest on the principal, that person would have a retirement income of approximately one hundred forty-three thousand dollars per year without touching the principal. If the person invested two thousand dollars per year ($5.48 a day), instead of one thousand dollars, starting at age twenty-five, the retirement principal would be almost 2.3 million dollars. The income on this amount would be approximately twenty-four thousand dollars per month or two hundred eighty-eight thousand dollars per year, without touching the principal.

With these examples in mind, you can set your financial investment goals. By determining the amount of income you would like to receive each month upon retirement, you can identify the amount of money you need to set aside each month.

One of the best ways to build a sound investment account is to use an IRA. The government will allow you to set aside two thousand dollars a year, tax free, if you meet certain qualifications. Your base income would be taxed after the deduction for the two thousand dollars. For example, if you earned twenty thousand dollars per year and you took an IRA deduction of two thousand dollars, you would pay taxes only on eighteen thousand dollars. Therefore, you would be saving on taxes as well as getting interest on your investment.

By using this approach, you would receive a better return from your IRA investment than if you were to invest after-tax dollars because you would receive interest on the full two thousand dollars. If you were to pay taxes on this amount at a 30 percent rate, you would only have fourteen hundred dollars to invest instead of the entire two thousand dollars.

The bottom line is that by being diligent and disciplined, the average individual can easily accumulate a retirement account in excess of one million dollars, just by setting aside a little from each paycheck and allowing compound interest to work.

When these principles are reviewed, it is easy to understand how the low-paid custodian could have accumulated enough to leave a substantial endowment to the charity of his choice upon his death.

Remember, if you spend less money than you earn, you will always have a surplus. The task, however, is to discipline yourself to live on 70 percent of your income. If you were to set living on 70 percent as a goal, you would be aiming at an objective that would automatically put you in control of your personal finances; you would always have a surplus to invest.

You must be faithful with what you have. You must start where you are. If you earn twelve thousand dollars per year, you must learn to live on less than twelve thousand dollars annually. If you don't learn to spend less than you earn, it won't make any difference if you earn twenty thousand dollars, fifty thousand dollars, or one hundred thousand dollars per year. Your spending would simply rise as your income rose.

Action Step

Spend less money than you earn,
and develop a surplus.

START NOW

According to the 1990 census, more than 75 percent of those who retire are retiring on less than ten thousand dollars annually, and more than 50 percent are retiring on less than five thousand dollars per year. I am sure that most of these people never intended to retire below the poverty level, but many made no preparation to avoid it.

You must start now and be diligent in order to use time and consistency in your favor. Table 3 shows that the sooner you get started, the better.

TABLE 3
Cost of Waiting to Invest

Starting Age	$1.00 per Day at 12% Interest	Cost to Wait
25	$296,516	$0
26	$264,402	$32,114
30	$116,858	$179,658

Cost of waiting from twenty-five to twenty-six years: $32,114.
Cost of waiting until age thirty: $179,658.

SHORT-TERM SAVINGS

Your short-term savings make up a holding account to cover your short-term goals. Some examples are:

1. Extra offerings to the church, giving to the poor, extending a helping hand to others, or other things the Lord may lay on your heart. Your offerings are always above and beyond your tithe. They can never be taken from your living expenses, or your entire budget will be thrown out of balance.

2. Your six months' emergency fund, which should cover six months' living expenses and other unexpected expenses.

3. Your savings and short-term purchases: auto, appliances, clothing, furniture, etc. Cut back on debt and interest expenses by planning ahead for purchases you will need in the future. Impulse buying and debt will be reduced to a minimum.

4. To provide coverage for higher deductibles on your auto, home, and health insurance. With a short-term savings account, you will substantially reduce your overall living expenses (see chapter 3, "Planning and Preparation").

```
┌─────────────────────────────────────┐
│             Action Step             │
│  Use your money market account to   │
│  store your short- and intermediate-│
│           term savings.             │
└─────────────────────────────────────┘
```

LONG-TERM SAVINGS

Since your long-term savings account is for long-term investments, this is your "do-not-touch money." The funds in this account should be used for the following items only:

1. to provide a retirement income (IRA, Keogh, mutual funds, annuities, etc.)

2. to create an estate (home, business, family support)

3. to meet other long-term goals, such as college for yourself and your children

Setting aside long-term savings is one of the most important steps the average family can take, but there is always the temptation to put it off until later. And once you do set aside some funds, there is the temptation to use this money for some short-term emergency.

To illustrate the point, let me tell you a personal story. Some time ago, when both my wife and I were working, we made a decision to open an annuity account. (An annuity is an insurance investment instrument in which you put money into your account for a specified time, leave the money in while it accumulates interest, and then take it out at a later time.) We faithfully paid into this account every month for five years. Then we ran into one of our regularly occurring "emergencies." After examining the circumstances, we decided that we would take the money out of our annuity account.

Because of my lack of understanding of financial planning, we made the same mistake that many families do. We sacrificed our long-term investments or savings for a short-term emergency. I found out later that this transaction was a costly mistake in a number of ways:

$ We lost our long-term investment. It would take a much larger monthly investment to get the same results the older we got.

$ We had paid a commission on the account, which reduced our initial investment.

$ We paid a penalty for early withdrawal.

$ We had to pay taxes on the money we received. (After five years, we actually had less money than we put in.)

Be careful to check out the terms of any investment or savings programs you are considering, to avoid these types of losses and penalties.

THE MONEY MOVEMENT STRATEGY

There is no such thing as a risk-free investment. An investment that makes a 60 percent return in one year can lose 80 percent in the next year. It is impossible to pick the top or bottom of a rising market. You can only use interest rates as an indicator to establish trends. The idea of the money movement strategy is to earn an average of 20 percent per year, pay no commission, and pay minimum taxes on your earnings.

This objective can be accomplished by using your IRA. You pay no commission up front when your IRA is invested in a no-load or rear-load mutual fund. Therefore, your account earns interest on your entire investment. There is, however, a small service charge by the money managers, whose cost is spread over the entire fund. With a rear-load mutual fund, you will pay a commission when you take your money out of your account. This may also be the case with a no-load mutual fund, depending on the type of fund you have. Moreover, you pay no taxes on your earnings until you withdraw your retirement fund at the age of a fifty-nine and a half.

Earning an average of 20 percent per year on your investment involves being in the right investment at the right time. As a rule, when interest rates are going down, you should have the majority of your investment in a bond mutual fund. When the current interest rate on the thirty-year treasury bond is below 8.5 percent, you should have most of your investments in a family of no-load or rear-load stock mutual funds. When the interest rate on the thirty-year bond rises above 8.5 percent, you should move the majority of your investment funds to the money market account in the same no-load mutual fund. You should have your account set up to include a telephone switching service so that these transactions can easily be accomplished. There are normally no commission charges for switching from stock, bonds, or money market funds in the same family.

You must be diligent in watching the change in long-term interest rates to receive the maximum benefits from this type of strategy. Otherwise, I suggest that you diversify in all three areas or get a broker whom you can trust to keep watch over your account if you don't have time.

Action Step

Use your no-load or rear-load mutual fund to finance your IRA and long-term investments.

FIFTEEN BIGGEST INVESTMENT MISTAKES

There are a number of things the average investor should avoid as a general rule. The list below shows you how to avoid the fifteen most common investment mistakes.

1. Never use life insurance as an investment. Buy life insurance to provide death benefits and to provide your survivors with immediate funds until your estate is settled.

2. Avoid individual stocks and bonds. Use a no-load or rear-load mutual fund for your investment needs. You pay no commission, and this approach takes a lot less time than researching individual stocks and bonds.

3. Never invest in bond funds when interest rates are rising.

4. Never buy investments over the phone from a broker you don't know.

5. Avoid buying stocks, bonds, and mutual funds from a brokerage house without comparing prices. Normally, you will pay very high commissions and unnecessary fees.

6. Never make an investment for tax savings alone.

7. Avoid borrowing money and using leverage funds to purchase stocks or bonds unless you have thoroughly researched the market and are an expert in that particular field.

8. Don't make any investments based on hunches and tips from friends, relatives, and anxious stockbrokers without totally understanding the investments.

9. Avoid switching your investments from one account to another more than once or twice a year. Market timing is critical in order to receive a 20 percent annual return, but unless you have time to watch the market on a consistent basis, this process is too time-consuming. Furthermore, each transaction by a commissioned broker costs you money. (Review the section on money movement strategy in this chapter.)

10. Avoid commissioned brokers unless they have demonstrated that they understand the principles and guidelines for finances set forth in the Bible and will assist you on a long-term basis to implement a sound, broad-based financial plan.

11. Never waste your money on time-sharing investment opportunities. Don't invest more than 5 to 10 percent of your investment portfolio in precious metals as a hedge (a means to protect yourself) against inflation.

12. Don't put your money into get-rich-quick investments, such as volatile commodities. Commodities operate on the same principle as stocks, but they involve perishable items, such as grain and beef.

13. Avoid investing in options. Options are contracts that allow you to buy or sell particular securities, commodities, or property interest at a specified price during a certain period of time. However, options are very risky types of investments, because you could lose all the money that you have put into them.

14. Unless you have a lot of money to invest, avoid overdiversification (dividing your money among securities of too many different industries or different classes). Choose the right type of mutual fund for the right economy.

15. Avoid buying expensive market-timing newsletters. No one knows when the market is going to go up or down on a week-to-week or month-to-month basis, unless that person is a money manager. Your main indicator should be the current long-term interest rate.

HOW TO CHOOSE A BROKER

It is important to follow these guidelines when choosing a broker or any other financial advisor:

1. Ask for the opinions of trusted friends who have dealt with no-load mutual funds in the past.

2. Identify an individual who understands no-load mutual funds and the value of term life insurance versus whole life insurance, and who will not try to pressure you into converting into a whole life policy several months later.

3. Try to locate a broker who understands biblical principles for handling money and who would be willing to use the key strategies listed in this chapter as a checklist to assist you in organizing your financial plan.

4. Become acquainted with the broker, but always compare his or her prices with other firms that have the same product.

5. It is all right to pay commission to a broker if the broker is willing to work with you on a consistent basis to keep your financial plan on track.

6. Take your time and make sure you understand every transaction. Don't be talked into purchases you don't understand.

7. Don't expect your broker to spend hours with you if you have a small account. Don't expect your broker to know when the stock market is going to go up or down. To conserve time, you should have your basic investment objectives clearly in mind before you call your broker.

IT'S OKAY TO HAVE AN INVESTMENT ACCOUNT

Remember that it is perfectly acceptable to have a surplus. The Bible teaches this principle in the Old and New Testaments. It is necessary to have a surplus to do what God asks you to do in regard to giving and meeting the needs of the poor. How can you give to God's work if you are living from paycheck to paycheck and not setting anything aside?

Action Step

Make a habit of paying yourself
first—after God.

We come back to the same principle: if you spend less than you earn, you will automatically have a surplus. You will have to store your surplus money somewhere. Recall that the Scriptures teach the importance of using resources wisely and the value of gaining interest. *"You should have put my money on deposit with the bankers, so that when I returned I would have received it back with interest"* (Matthew 25:27 NIV). Therefore, it is okay to have investments. It is also acceptable to receive interest on your investments.

Action Step

Organize your surplus account to reflect the call that God has put on your life.

MONEY: THE ROOT OF ALL EVIL?

Many people are confused because they have the misconception that money is inherently bad. Money is neither good nor evil. However, a common myth that has been passed down through religious tradition is that money is the root of all evil. This is not what the Bible teaches. It actually says, *"For the love of money is the root of all evil"* (1 Timothy 6:10).

The Scripture states clearly that it is the *love* of money that is the cause of all kinds of evil. Money is not evil in itself. This Scripture has been grossly misquoted over the years. As a result, it has driven many individuals away from Christianity.

When I was a youngster living with my grandparents, I heard this Scripture quoted incorrectly throughout the Christian community. My grandfather was a minister, and he lived a simple lifestyle. Since the church was small, the collections were always limited. I noticed that the largest bill in the offering plate at church was usually a dollar. My grandparents and all the people whom I remember from my childhood were poor. Therefore, in spite of the fact that I had a good upbringing by my Christian grandparents, I grew up thinking that to be a good Christian, you had to be poor.

This is not the attitude we should have as Christians. If money were the root of all evil, a good Christian would logically not want to be associated with money. However, the truth is that money will take on the character of whomever has it. If you are a good Christian, your checkbook will reflect it. A good person will spend his or her money in a way that reflects godly character. Likewise, an evil person's spending will reflect his or her character. It is not the money that is good or bad, but what a person is willing to do to get it or what a person does with it after receiving it.

A faithful steward learns how money works. A faithful steward knows how to get a return on an investment. In Matthew 25, the two faithful stewards were rewarded because they had doubled their master's resources. According to the Bible, it is wise to save for the future: *"The wise man saves for the future, but the foolish man spends whatever he gets"* (Proverbs 21:20 TLB).

The ant is wise because he stores food in the summer to survive the winter (Proverbs 6:6–8). The summer of your life is when you are young and have time on your side. It is the season when you should begin investing so that compound interest can have the greatest impact on your finances. Unfortunately, however, this is also the time when people have the greatest appetite for consumption.

You should make a habit of saving. If necessary, you should force yourself to be thrifty. One way this can be done is through a payroll deduction plan at work or through your credit union. By having your savings taken off the top, you won't be tempted to spend your retirement.

AVOID SPECULATIVE INVESTMENTS

Investments can cover a variety of areas. Never invest in any venture that you don't understand. The Bible says you should avoid speculative investments:

There is another serious problem I have seen everywhere— savings are put into risky investments that turn sour, and soon there is nothing left to pass on to one's son. The man who speculates is soon back to where he began—with nothing. This, as I said, is a very serious problem, for all his hard work has been for nothing; he has been working for the wind. It is all swept away. (Ecclesiastes 5:13–16 TLB)

The cause of most bad investments is greed, the thought of a quick buck, desiring a large return on something you have not worked to earn. Nevertheless, one hears constant reports of people who have lost their money trying to get a quick return.

Action Step

Avoid risky investments and
get-rich-quick schemes.

YOUR BEST INVESTMENT

The best investment you can make is in the kingdom of God:

Tell those who are rich not to be proud and not to trust in their money, which will soon be gone, but their pride and trust should be in the living God who always richly gives us all we need for our enjoyment. Tell them to use their money to do good. They should be rich in good works and should give happily to those in need, always being ready to share with others whatever God has given them. By doing this they will be storing up real treasure for themselves in heaven—it is the only safe investment for eternity! And they will be living a fruitful Christian life down here as well. (1 Timothy 6:17–19 TLB)

He gives generously to those in need. His deeds will never be forgotten. He shall have influence and honor.
(Psalm 112:9 TLB)

You can invest in your heavenly account by sharing with others the resources with which God has blessed you here on earth.

Action Step

Make investments that will pay an
eternal return.

PRACTICAL APPLICATION

To start to build wealth in God's financial system, you must
act on the principles outlined in this chapter. Contact your investment advisor or financial planner, and let him or her know
that you want to implement the twenty-one practical steps to
building wealth in God's economy that are outlined in chapter
12.

CHAPTER 9

ELIMINATING WASTE

Ye have sown much, and bring in little; ye eat, but ye have not enough; ye drink, but ye are not filled with drink; ye clothe you, but there is none warm; and he that earneth wages earneth wages to put it into a bag with holes. Thus saith the LORD of hosts; Consider your ways.
—Haggai 1:6–7

And he said also unto his disciples, There was a certain rich man, which had a steward; and the same was accused unto him that he had wasted his goods. And he called him, and said unto him, How is it that I hear this of thee? give an account of thy stewardship; for thou mayest be no longer steward.
—Luke 16:1–2

On my way to the church service following Sunday school one morning, John Davis, one of my former students, approached me. He had been through my basic money management class about six months earlier.

"I just wanted to let you know that the lesson you gave on how to save money on insurance was very helpful to me," John said.

I remembered that he had been enthusiastic about the material presented during the course.

"What part of that lesson proved beneficial?" I asked.

"When I checked on my car insurance to look for duplication of unnecessary coverage, as you suggested, I was shocked at what I found. First of all, I had a good company-sponsored health plan where I worked that would cover any hospital bills, whether they were caused by an auto accident or not.

"I decided to drop the duplicate coverage in my car insurance, since the insurance company will not pay benefits for medical expenses if they have already been paid by another company. Then, by raising my deductible from fifty dollars to five hundred dollars on comprehensive and collision, this premium also dropped."

"Great!" I said. "How much did you save?"

With a big smile, John answered, "Forty dollars per month on my car insurance alone."

"What did you do with the forty dollars per month that you saved?"

"I took the money and bought a new boat that I couldn't afford before," John said.

His response did not surprise me. This is a typical attitude toward spending that we should guard against as wise stewards. John probably did not buy a new boat for forty dollars. It is more likely that he bought the new boat on credit and increased his debt payments by forty dollars per month. Instead of adding to his surplus, he added to his monthly expenditures.

There is nothing wrong with purchasing a boat. However, one of the most common responses I receive from workshop participants across the country is that they don't have enough money to open a savings or investment account or to pay off their existing debt.

This chapter will examine ways by which you can find money in your current budget to use for savings and investments or for your surplus account. By eliminating waste, you can continually discover ways to find more money in your budget with no increase in your income—even if you have a modest income.

SEWING UP THE HOLE IN YOUR FINANCIAL POCKET

In the last chapter, I discussed how you can develop a 20 percent surplus from existing income and how compound interest works, along with key investment strategies and how they fit into developing a sound financial plan.

In this chapter, I will describe how you can take control of your personal finances with the use of a family budget and by eliminating waste from your disposable income. By eliminating waste and making prudent purchases, you can make your current income go much further. Your goal is to reorganize your spending habits so that you can live on a maximum of 70 percent of your income, after you develop your surplus.

With these objectives in mind, now you can set your family's financial goals and establish a realistic family budget.

The best way to reduce the amount of money you spend each month is to divide your spending into separate components and then identify ways to reduce spending in each area. Examine the sample family budget in figure 5 at the end of the chapter. It outlines each spending category and also sets upper and lower targets to help you evaluate your situation. Figure 6 provides a form for you to list your financial goals. Since planning and preparation are keys to success, figure 6 also includes a form you can use to write down what you will do this month and this week, to start yourself on the road to financial freedom. The following information will show you how to do this.

THE BUDGET: YOUR PLAN OF ACTION

In order to effectively take control of your personal finances, you need to write out your financial goals. This process begins with establishing a family budget. A budget is a written plan in which you take your existing circumstances into account—your current income and expenses. Your written plan also should include a current financial statement and a list of your goals. From there, your budget becomes a plan of action by which you can get the maximum benefits from your existing income. It allows you to set priorities in regard to spending.

Action Step

Establish a family budget to set
spending priorities.

Budgeting may not be the most anticipated activity on your family's agenda; however, it is the only way that you will be able to apply biblical principles to your lives. It is the only way you can put into practical application the principles of getting out of debt, saving and investing, and giving to the needy, and still be able to meet basic family needs.

Unfortunately, fundamental self-control is not an automatic part of the average American makeup. Unless it has an organized plan for spending, the average family will have problems with overspending.

Again, a budget allows you to take control of your personal finances. Remember, it's not the amount of money you earn that matters; it's how you manage what you have. I have talked to individuals earning twelve thousand dollars per year who weren't able to make ends meet. I have talked to individuals who could not live on forty thousand dollars per year. And I have talked to individuals earning over one hundred thousand dollars per year who could not live on their salaries.

Action Step

Keep to your budget, and learn to
live within your means.

Learn how to live on what you earn. Yes, the secret is living within your means. As I wrote in chapter 8, "Changing Surplus into Abundance," if you spend less than you make, you will always have a surplus. Unless you implement a budget, your expenses will invariably outpace your income. Budgeting allows you to take the impulse out of your spending. It allows you to develop control over your spending habits.

Action Step

Set priorities for your spending
according to your financial goals and
your budget.

How to Start Your Budget

Prepare your monthly budget by writing down your income and a detailed list of your family's monthly expenses. In order for a budget to be effective, you must be able to use it. It must be a tool that allows you to manage your family's finances. Many people have taken the effort to start a budget but have discontinued it because it did not make provision for unexpected necessities such as clothes, dentists, doctors, and entertainment.

Action Step

Make your budget, and stick to it.

Therefore, to start your budget, you must determine where you are at present. What is your current situation? You must determine how much you earn and how much money you spend each month. You must keep proper records.

This step is usually the most difficult because the majority of families tend to underestimate their expenses. Most people don't really know what they spend each month on simple items such as eating out and miscellaneous expenses that aren't payable on a monthly basis.

Action Step

Run all your income through your
checking account.

To prepare an accurate budget, you must account for every dime you spend. The easiest way to take control of your spending is to use your checking account to pay for major purchases. Then carry a small notebook to keep track of smaller purchases. This should be done for at least a month to establish current spending habits in order to estimate your preliminary budget.

In chapter 4, "Dealing with the Bondage of Debt," I discussed the dangers of falling into the trap of surety. Remember what the Scriptures say about this pitfall:

He who puts up security for another will surely suffer, but whoever refuses to strike hands in pledge is safe.
(Proverbs 11:15)

My son, if you become surety for your friend, if you have shaken hands in pledge for a stranger, you are snared by the words of your mouth; you are taken by the words of your mouth. So do this, my son, and deliver yourself; for you have come into the hand of your friend: go and humble yourself; plead with your friend. Give no sleep to your eyes, nor slumber to your eyelids. Deliver yourself like a gazelle from the hand of the hunter, and like a bird from the hand of the fowler. (Proverbs 6:1–5 NKJV)

A budget is in balance when income is larger than expenditures. If you are spending more money than you earn, your budget is out of balance. You are already in a surety position, or you are *rapidly* approaching it. There are only two ways to balance a budget: increase your income, or decrease your expenditures.

In order to increase your income, you could get a part-time job or establish a part-time business. Once you gain additional income, however, it is important that the extra income be applied toward getting the family budget balanced and not toward increased spending.

SET FAMILY FINANCIAL GOALS

The best way to get God involved in your personal finances is to organize your plans according to biblical principles. Remember, the only difference between Christians and non-Christians, in relation to personal finances, is what they are willing to do to get money and what they actually do with their money after they get it!

> **Action Step**
>
> Make your budget, and stick to it.
> Set a goal to live on 70 percent of
> your income.

To establish a financial plan, you must set family financial goals. You can't have everything. You must set priorities. Budgeting must be a family effort. Set a goal to live on 70 percent of your current income. This process will allow the family an opportunity to establish open communications in setting priorities.

The most effective way to begin this process is for the husband and wife to ask each other questions about their long-term goals and desires. What do you want to accomplish in life? What are your priorities as a family? What will your number one spending priority be? Will you put God first? What will your second-highest priority be—setting aside funds for retirement, getting out of debt, or just being able to get by until next month? You may be surprised at the answers you come up with.

> **Action Step**
>
> Decide where you want to be in five
> to ten years, and set financial goals
> to get there.

I suggest that families pray before they start the process of setting financial goals. Husbands and wives should then begin by answering specific financial questions individually. Once they have answered the questions, they should come together and compare their lists. This is where adjustment and agreement must take place. If one spouse is too far to one side on an issue, he or she should drop back to a point where both can agree. No decisions on spending money should be made unless both partners are in agreement on the purchase. If there is no agreement, no purchase should be made. Husbands and wives should, of course, be supportive of one other. Remember that the purpose of this exercise is to bring the family closer together in accomplishing financial objectives.

Set the priorities that mean the most to you. Your budget will allow you to take control of your circumstances instead of letting them control you.

Here are some sample questions that you can use to help determine your financial goals:

FINANCIAL GOALS QUESTIONS

1. What are the most important things that you would like to accomplish?

2. What long-term financial goals would you like to achieve in ten to twenty years? How much do you want to set aside for long-term savings?

3. What financial goals would you like to achieve within the next five to ten years?

4. What financial goals would you like to accomplish next year?

5. Do you communicate clearly with your spouse about financial matters?

6. What are your educational plans for the children?

7. What are your retirement goals?

8. What are your giving goals (to the Gospel and the poor)?

9. What is your goal concerning debt and interest payments?

10. What do you want to give to your local church?

PUT YOUR FINANCIAL GOALS IN WRITING

If you want to get the best results, your goals should be in writing. *"Then the LORD answered me and said: "Write the vision and make it plain on tablets, that he may run who reads it"* (Habakkuk 2:2 NKJV). By establishing written goals, your family will learn how to set priorities. The process will allow you to identify the objectives that you feel are most important to the family.

Again, they should be prepared with input from each family member. As I wrote earlier, these exercises will help to bring the family closer together. They will establish a solid channel of communication between husband and wife. And, with input from the children, parents can identify realistic family goals and give everyone on the same focus. After receiving the suggestions from the other members of the family, the husband and wife should set final priorities.

There are several things that you should do in establishing your family financial aims:

1. Understand fundamental biblical principles that govern your finances. Then, incorporate these principles as you organize your overall goals. (Refer to the strategies for creating a surplus and building a sound financial foundation that are outlined in chapter 8.)

2. Both husband and wife should write out individual goals separately. Then the children should do the same.

3. After each individual writes his or her personal goals, the husband and wife should compile the family's goals.

Examples of goals that you and your family may want to accomplish are:

$ buying a new house
$ college for the children
$ having a retirement fund
$ buying a new automobile

These goals may be divided into long-term and short-term objectives. One goal may have a higher priority for your family than another goal.

Be realistic in establishing your goals. Make the goals practical. If you set your goals too far out into the future, where you really don't believe you can accomplish them, they are unrealistic and will hinder your overall financial plan. The next step is to take your long-term and intermediate goals and break them into bite-sized chunks, which can be handled on a month-to-month basis. And finally, you should use a daily "Things to Do" list. This list should consist of what comes up during the week, but priority should be given to those items that are consistent with your long-term and intermediate goals.

GUIDELINES FOR BALANCING YOUR BUDGET

Once your financial goals are set, you can concentrate on achieving them. This may be accomplished by eliminating waste so that you can begin saving for them. The best way to reduce the amount of money you spend each month is to divide each of your budget categories into separate components and then identify ways to reduce spending in each area. The main areas of expense are:

$ housing
$ food
$ transportation (car purchase and upkeep)
$ clothing
$ insurance and medical expenses
$ entertainment and recreation
$ miscellaneous
$ debt reduction

Housing

The expenses in this category are house payments, maintenance, lawn upkeep, taxes and insurance, telephone, and other utilities. Your housing expenses should be between 25 and 30 percent of your net income. Use the following guidelines to help you reduce your expenses in this area:

1. When purchasing a home, the best buy is an older house or a foreclosure. Make sure your house is adequate for your living needs today but don't buy a house that is larger than you need, with plans to expand into it.

2. Examine your interest rate, and refinance if there are two points or more between it and the current rate. For example,

if you have a thirty-year mortgage for one hundred thousand dollars at 10.5 percent interest, you can save more than two hundred dollars per month by refinancing it at 8 to 8.5 percent. You also can purchase a fifteen-year mortgage for a few dollars more per month. Check with your local mortgage company for options.

3. Consider doing maintenance and upkeep yourself—lawn care, pest control, painting, and carpet cleaning.

4. Examine your current homeowners' insurance and compare the price with three other insurance companies. Increasing your deductible could substantially reduce your premium.

5. Lower your utility bills by installing ceiling fans and by limiting your use of heat, lights, and air-conditioning.

6. Never buy furniture and appliances on credit when trying to reduce your expenses. Use garage sales and used appliance stores to obtain reasonable prices on household goods and appliances, or pay for them with cash from your surplus account. Newspaper advertisements are a useful source for locating good buys.

7. Write letters or use E-mail instead of making long-distance telephone calls.

Food

This category includes groceries, sundry items, and eating out. Food expenses should not exceed 15 to 20 percent of the family budget. This area requires definite planning in order to reap benefits.

1. The best way to cut food expenses is to plan your daily menus at least an entire week ahead of time.

2. Once you have established what you will serve, make a list of items that will support the menu. When you go shopping, always use a written list to avoid impulse buying.

3. Make your grocery list for an entire week to conserve gas and limit unnecessary trips to the market. Reduce or eliminate junk food and ready-to-eat items, such as sugar-coated cereal, TV dinners, pot pies, and cakes.

4. Avoid going shopping when you are hungry. Leave children and hungry spouses at home; they will always pressure you to buy things that are not on your list.

5. Always pay attention as the clerk rings up your items, and double-check your receipt. If an item does not ring up correctly, bring it to the attention of the store manager. Sale prices are sometimes left out of the store's computer.

6. Consider canning fresh fruits and vegetables whenever possible. Save glass jars for this purpose from products you buy.

7. Make lunches for your spouse and children to reduce lunch expenses.

8. Reduce your use of disposable items, such as paper towels, plates, cups, and napkins. These can be more expensive than you think.

Transportation

Automobile payments, gasoline, and maintenance are included in this category, which should not exceed 10 to 15 percent of your net income. The main purpose of an automobile is transportation. Many families, however, have been trapped into buying cars they cannot afford because they view automobiles as status symbols.

1. Keep the automobile you have. It is better to repair an automobile that still has miles of use left in it than to purchase a new one and be locked into monthly payments. The average American car will last from five to seven years with proper maintenance. Many will last much longer.

2. Buy a low-cost used car and drive it until it can no longer be maintained inexpensively.

3. Take care of your automobile. Change the oil every twenty-five hundred to three thousand miles, especially with city driving.

4. When purchasing a new automobile, it is best to wait for the sales at the end of the model year.

5. Purchase a two-year-old car from a wholesaler. Look for a model that will continue to have the current body style for a number of years. Usually, this method will allow you to buy a low-mileage car at up to 50 percent of its original value.

6. Pay cash for your car when possible. Use your short-term savings account (surplus account) to accumulate the cash.

7. Never take credit life insurance when financing a car. The cost is more than 500 percent higher than purchasing insurance directly from an insurance company.

Clothing

This category should not exceed 4 to 5 percent of your net income. Many families with limited income spend more money than they should in this area. They are held hostage by fads. Sporting outfits, for example, are astronomically priced.

1. Make an annual budget for clothing needs. Make a list of items you need and purchase them in the off-season. Shop at economical and discount stores and garage sales. You can end up with designer labels at a good price if you shop carefully.

2. Educate family members about caring for their clothing and other possessions. Teach everyone how to do the laundry in order to keep clothing in shape.

Insurance and Medical Expenses

Insurance and medical expenses should not exceed 7 to 10 percent of your budget.

1. Never take the minimum deductible of fifty to one hundred dollars on your insurance. Increase your deductible to five hundred or one thousand dollars and save as much as 50 percent on your automobile insurance.

2. Use your company's group health insurance policy when possible. Use a higher deductible to cut costs and still be covered for major illness. Cover yourself for the higher deductible with the emergency funds in your surplus account.

3. Practice preventive medicine. It is much better to maintain a healthy body than to pay additional money on doctor bills. See that you and your family practice proper nutrition, exercise, and get enough rest. Get regular checkups and the recommended tests at the appropriate ages.

4. Reduce dental bills by practicing proper dental hygiene and having regular checkups. Take care of minor problems before they become major ones.

Note: A more detailed discussion on insurance is included in the next chapter.

Vacations and Recreation

This category covers vacation and recreational activities. You should not spend more than 3 to 5 percent of your disposable income on this area.

1. Plan to take vacations during the off-season. This will significantly reduce the cost.

2. Reduce recreational spending by taking vacations closer to home or in less trendy spots.

3. Consider the possibility of taking camping vacations to avoid motel and restaurant expenses. When you do stay in a motel, pack the ice chest, and eat one meal per day in your room.

4. Vacation packages often offer the best buys. Many include transportation, lodging, and some meals.

5. When taking children along, remember that many educational activities, such as visiting museums, parks, and historical sites, are fun and inexpensive.

Miscellaneous

Gifts, entertainment, school expenses, and allowances are included under "miscellaneous." This category should not amount to more than 3 to 5 percent of your income.

1. When purchasing gifts for Christmas, have the family agree on limits. Instead of gifts, ask relatives to give cash that you can use to lower the principal on your debt.
2. Purchase gifts, Christmas decorations, and other holiday items during the off-season and stash them in a closet until needed. Gifts can be prewrapped and labeled for "emergencies."
3. Set allowances for both adults and children. This area is a real budget buster; therefore, it is necessary to make provisions at budget-setting time for the husband and wife to have money to spend on personal items.

Debt Reduction

This part of your expenses (for interest and principal payments) should not consume more than 10 percent of your income.

1. Establish a debt-reduction plan, and set a goal to eliminate interest payments.
2. Pay all credit cards in full at the end of each month or destroy them.
3. Always avoid surety in your personal finances. If you make twelve thousand dollars or less, you can't afford to purchase items on credit. Principal and interest payments are sure budget-busters.

HOW TO SAVE ON TAXES

Families may also be able to save money in the area of taxes. Individuals must be responsible for carrying out appropriate research into tax laws and keeping necessary records, while feeling comfortable with the actions they are taking. Christians, furthermore, must always handle business affairs with honesty and integrity.

Obviously, because tax reduction is a complex area, it cannot be covered in detail here. But there are two very beneficial steps that the average family can take that will have a direct impact on their tax burden:

1. IRA (individual retirement account): The average family is allowed to take two thousand dollars off the top of their income and put it directly into a retirement account. With a few restrictions, this transition is completely tax deferred for the average wage earner. For example, if you earn twenty thousand dollars per year, you will pay tax on only eighteen thousand dollars for the year that you invest two thousand dollars in an IRA. If you select a reputable no-load or rear-load mutual fund, your retirement account will receive compound interest on the pre-tax dollar until you retire.

2. Small-business deductions: If you start and operate a small business, you are allowed to deduct the expenses of the business. It is important that you understand the tax regulations and are willing to keep proper records. Check with your local Internal Revenue Service (IRS) office for their circular on small businesses.

GET SERIOUS ABOUT YOUR FINANCIAL SITUATION

Because of impulse buying, many Americans have been caught in the trap of wasting their financial resources without ever realizing it. Moreover, because of the Madison Avenue mentality, we are not only buying things on impulse, but we are also buying things that we don't really need, and we are paying too much for them because of the use of credit.

To eliminate waste, you must reduce your current spending habits to establish a surplus. You should set the direction in which your money flows—not the Madison Avenue advertiser, your friends and neighbors, or any set of false attitudes that presently define success. Our standards of success should be defined by God's Word. Impulse buying is a sign of lack of discipline and self-control over lust and personal desires. This habit is a true indicator of the power and control that the world economy has over our lives.

Remember, it is not the amount of money you bring in, but the amount of money you keep that counts. What is important is how much you can reduce your current expenditures in relation to the amount that you earn.

PRACTICAL APPLICATION

$ Develop your family budget and financial goals by using the forms (figures 5 and 6) provided at the end of this chapter.

$ If you are serious about applying biblical money management principles to your personal finances, I suggest that you ask your pastor to set up classes to teach biblical principles of basic money management and/or let your church select a person who will take this on as a ministry.

FIGURE 5
Family Budget

Income Per Month

Salary _____

Rental Property _____

Other _____

Other _____

Other _____

Total Income _____

(less) Taxes _____

Net Income _____

_____

**Net Monthly Income
(from above)**

_____

**Total Expenses
(from list at right)**

_____

Total Savings

_____

*Note: Have your
savings deducted
directly from your
paycheck (payroll
deduction) if possible.*

**If you spend
less than you
earn, you will
always have
a surplus.**

Payments Per Month

1. Tithe (10%) _____
2. Personal Savings (20%) _____
   A. Short-term _____
   B. Long-term _____
3. Debt Repayment (0–10%) _____
   Major Loan _____
   Credit Card _____
   Installments_____
   Other_____
4. Housing (25–30%) _____
   A. Payments (or Rent) _____
   B. Lawn _____
   C. Maintenance_____
   D. Taxes and Insurance _____
   E. Telephone _____
   F. Electricity _____
   G. Gas _____
   H. Water_____
   I. Garbage _____
5. Food (15–20%)_____
   A. Groceries_____
   B. Sundry Items _____
   C. Eating Out _____
6. Auto (10–15%)_____
   A. Payments _____
   B. Gasoline_____
   C. Maintenance_____
7. Insurance (3–5%) _____
   A. Auto _____
   B. Health _____
   C. Life _____
   D. Other _____
8. Entertainment/Recreation (3–5%) _____
9. Clothing (4–5%) _____
10. Medical (4–5%) _____
    A. Dentist_____
    B. Doctor _____
    C. Other _____
11. Miscellaneous (3–5%)_____
    A. Gifts _____
    B. Vacation_____
    C. Education _____
    D. Allowances _____
    E. Other _____

FIGURE 6
This Year's Financial Goals

1. _____
2. _____
3. _____
4. _____
5. _____
6. _____
7. _____
8. _____
9. _____
10. _____
11. _____
12. _____
13. _____
14. _____
15. _____
16. _____
17. _____
18. _____
19. _____
20. _____
21. _____
22. _____
23. _____
24. _____
25. _____

FIGURE 6, continued

Goals to Fulfill This Month

1. _____
2. _____
3. _____
4. _____
5. _____
6. _____
7. _____
8. _____
9. _____
10. _____

Goals to Fulfill This Week

1. _____
2. _____
3. _____
4. _____
5. _____

CHAPTER 10

SAVING MONEY ON INSURANCE

The purpose of insurance is to act as a safety net, not as protection. Your protection is in the Lord (see Psalm 91). Life insurance should be used to replace the income of the major breadwinner in case of death. Other types of insurance should be purchased so that you can repair or replace damaged or lost property.

I stated earlier that the average individual can reduce insurance costs by as much as 50 percent. This chapter will explain how.

Most insurance is sold on the basis of fear. "If something should happen, you would want to protect your loved ones, wouldn't you?" the salesperson asks. The more you think about the consequences from an emotional standpoint, the more insurance you purchase that you don't really need. However, with a closer look at the facts, you can eliminate much of your confusion regarding insurance. Many families spend up to one-third of their income on interest and insurance. But your total insurance cost does not need to come to more than 5 percent of your total income.

Insurance can be divided into these categories: auto, life, homeowners', health, and other. The following is a look at each type.

AUTOMOBILE INSURANCE

Automobile insurance can be one of the most costly categories. It is part of casualty insurance, a term that covers everything other than life insurance. There are three basic areas of automobile insurance: liability, comprehensive, and collision.

Liability Insurance

Liability insurance covers damages to someone else's person or property. If you were to accidentally hit someone's automobile, your liability policy would pay to repair the other person's car. If someone were hurt, it would cover expenses for the treatment of that person's injuries. There are three basic types of liability insurance: bodily injury, property damage liability, and umbrella liability.

Bodily injury liability insurance covers people in the other car, passengers in the policyholder's car, and the policyholder, even when he or she is driving someone else's car or a rental car. Bodily injury insurance also covers legal defense damage up to the limit of the policy.

Most states require a minimum of $10,000 to $20,000 in liability coverage. This means that the policyholder is covered for ten thousand dollars per person up to a maximum of twenty thousand dollars per accident.

Now, how much bodily liability insurance should you carry? This may vary from family to family. If you rent and don't own any property and live from paycheck to paycheck, you probably can get by with the minimum. If you have from fifty thousand to one hundred thousand dollars of equity in your home, personal assets, retirement accounts, etc., you might want to consider increasing your coverage in the range of $250,000 to $500,000.

How much property damage liability should you cover? Keep in mind that property damage liability covers damages to someone else's car or property caused by the policyholder's car. This insurance covers your family and anyone you give permission to drive your car. To properly cover yourself, you should consider the current cost of automobiles or the cost of two or three (in case of a pileup). You should consider a minimum of at least fifty thousand dollars or a maximum of one hundred thousand dollars per accident.

In most cases, you will pay higher premiums if there is a teenager in your family who drives.

What about umbrella liability coverage? This is a liability policy sold by home and automobile insurance companies.

Because of high court costs and the proliferation of lawsuits, everyone with reasonable assets is concerned about a lawsuit. Yet, in most cases, your insurance agent won't mention an umbrella policy to you because it's inexpensive and pays him or her only a small commission. It varies from company to company, but the cost is usually between one hundred and one hundred fifty dollars per year for one million dollars of coverage. Usually you get the best price when you get both homeowners' and auto insurance from the same company issuing the umbrella policy. You should have between one hundred thousand and three hundred thousand dollars in coverage. Instead of doubling the coverage on both your home and auto insurance, you should add a one-hundred-thousand-dollar umbrella policy to complete your liability coverage.

Comprehensive Insurance

The comprehensive policy takes up where the liability policy leaves off. While liability insurance takes care of damage or injury to someone else's car or property, comprehensive insurance covers your car or property.

Comprehensive insurance pays for losses such as theft, fire damage, windshield and glass breakage, hail damage, and damage from falling objects. The minimum deductible ranges from fifty to one hundred dollars, depending on the company.

Collision Insurance

Collision insurance also covers damage to your car. No matter who is at fault, if you collide with another vehicle, you will be covered under a collision package. If the other driver is at fault, your insurance company will seek reimbursement from the other driver's insurance company. The deductible for collision insurance ranges from one hundred to one thousand dollars.

SAVE 40 TO 50 PERCENT ON CAR INSURANCE

There are many ways to reduce the cost of your automobile insurance. The major ways are outlined below.

1. Increase your deductible on your comprehensive coverage from the standard fifty dollars to five hundred or one thousand dollars. You will save as much as 50 percent in some cases.

2. Avoid double coverage. You cannot collect on the same medical expenses twice, no matter how many insurance companies cover you. However, before doing this, look carefully at all your policies to make sure you will be adequately covered.

3. Avoid uninsured motorist coverage. This is usually a duplicate coverage since any damage done to your auto will be covered by your auto insurance and any bodily injury will be covered by your hospitalization policy.

4. Avoid no-fault insurance unless it is required by the state in which you live. In most cases, this is a double-coverage insurance.

5. Eliminate insurance you don't need. When your car drops below a certain value, your insurance company will pay you only the market value of your car no matter how much you pay for comprehensive and collision. It's cheaper to insure it yourself.

6. Avoid rental car insurance. Rental car insurance is often covered on your credit card, and you are covered under your auto insurance and hospitalization. Rental car insurance is almost always double coverage.

7. Avoid special TV and mail-order insurance. Most mail-order insurance is expensive. It is usually marked up 400 to 500 percent to cover expensive advertising.

8. Avoid extended warranties. Extended warranties are available from retail outlets for automobiles and appliances. These insurance policies normally cover your appliances or

car through the warranty period for a certain length of time. You should look at this type of coverage and make up your own mind. It is normally expensive, and many times it is never used. But I have seen cases involving new appliances and ice-maker refrigerators in which this warranty has come in handy. For the most part, you will save money by eliminating extended warranties on most household products.

Action Step

Ask for automobile insurance discounts.

DROPPED OR LAPSED POLICIES

Do not let your auto policy lapse, and do not drop your coverage before you establish coverage with another company. An example from my own life applies. At one point, our family had an unexpected reduction in income. To compensate, we cut everything to the bare necessities. We decided to let our automobile insurance premium slide for a few months.

As business began to pick up, we went back to our insurance company to reinstate coverage on our automobiles. When we contacted our agent, he informed us that we could not renew our policy under its previous conditions. When I asked why, he said that it had been more than thirty days since the policy had expired. Therefore, our family would have to start over as a new customer with no previous insurance record.

"Okay," I said. "What is the additional cost going to be?"

"That will be twelve hundred dollars for the first six months."

"What! Twelve hundred dollars? Before, our policy was only $275 for six months. Are you telling me that the cost of the same policy will increase more than 400 percent, even though I have the same clean driving record?"

"Yes, that is the way it is," he said. "You will have to pay this insurance premium for the first year, and then your insurance premium will decrease by 10 percent if you maintain a good driving record."

Needless to say, I was very disturbed over this development. It would have been better for me to have dropped all other coverage and kept simple liability coverage on my automobile than to have dropped the entire coverage. The same principle applies if you have a series of accidents or traffic violations, because your rates will skyrocket.

Action Step

Always make sure your replacement automobile policy has a better overall return before you cancel any existing policy.

CHOOSE YOUR INSURANCE AGENT WISELY

In many cases, people buy insurance from a person they know and trust. They believe that this person is looking out for their best interests. They feel that the agent understands their particular circumstances.

However, if you do not know your options and you let your guard down, the temptation for the agent to make a commission will be too great. Often, the agent will sell you the policy that will make the most commission for him or her and long-term cash flow for the company.

A wise steward understands how the system works and shops around to keep insurance and investment brokers honest. A wise steward carefully directs his or her dollars and pays only a fair commission for services needed.

I suggest that you get a sound financial adviser or broker who understands both insurance (automobile and life) and investments (no-load mutual funds). Review the guidelines from chapter 8 on choosing this adviser.

LIFE INSURANCE

Let me reemphasize that overspending on insurance combined with interest on debt can consume as much as one-third of the average family's income. Of course, this amount varies from family to family. Yet, many who purchase insurance primarily take the word of their agents and usually buy more than they need. This section will take a closer look at life insurance to see where waste can be eliminated.

Life insurance is an institutional plan by which an insurance company allows you to pay certain amounts of money while you are living so that you can leave money to someone you care for after you die. The main purpose of life insurance is to protect your family or loved ones from financial disaster if you should die. You want them to live basically the same lifestyle they had before your death.

Life insurance is excellent for this purpose, but you must understand how basic life insurance works in order to accomplish this purpose wisely. The following are some of the basic terms associated with life insurance. Knowing these terms will help you to understand how to make proper decisions regarding your own life insurance.

Death Benefit

The death benefit is the amount of money the insurance company will pay the beneficiary when the insured person dies. This is also called the *face value* of the insurance policy. It is the amount of payment for life insurance that will be received by your loved ones.

Term of the Policy

This is the time period in which the life insurance is in force. The term of the policy can be any amount of time (one year, ten years, twenty years, a lifetime).

Premium

The premium is the amount of money you pay the insurance company to keep your life insurance policy in force. Premiums can be paid in a number of different ways—monthly, semiannually, annually, and sometimes in lump-sum single premiums. Most policies are paid for in quarterly or monthly installments.

There are at least four instances in which you should not purchase life insurance:

$ Never buy insurance on children.

$ If you have no dependents and no assets, you do not need life insurance. Your savings or investments can be used to cover your funeral expenses (see section in this chapter on "Individual Insurance with No Dependents and No Assets").

$ Do not buy education policies for your children.

$ Never purchase life insurance as an investment.

Insurance on Children

Regarding life insurance for children, remember that the purpose of life insurance is to protect your family against the loss of your financial assets when you die. Children are not financial assets.

Many parents are persuaded to buy life insurance on their children by salespeople whom they feel know best. And these salespeople often tell parents that buying insurance for their children is a responsible thing to do. The usual line is, "You love your children, don't you? Therefore, you should insure them."

The main point that the salesperson does not mention is that the longer you are in a whole life policy, the more money the company and salesperson make. The longer a person lives, the more insurance premiums he or she pays. Salespeople will tell you that you should insure children while they are young so that they will be guaranteed to be eligible for insurance later. Yet, according to statistics, more than 99 percent of teenagers are eligible for insurance at age eighteen.

Individual Insurance with No Dependents and No Assets

Also, by looking at the statistics, we find that about 30 percent of the life insurance policies that are in effect are on the lives of unmarried people with no family obligations. They have purchased insurance because insurance companies have convinced them that everyone should have life insurance.

Life insurance should be used only to prevent financial loss and hardship to the beneficiary after a person dies. Why would a person without dependents or a family buy life insurance? To whom would he or she leave the proceeds?

Always remember that the purpose of life insurance is to protect the ones who are left. It would be more appropriate for people to invest in a mutual fund that would produce more interest income and give them burial coverage if something unexpected happened.

Insurance Policy for College

An education life insurance policy is one of the lowest interest-paying investment accounts available. You should never mix investment and insurance in the same package. The insurance company will always win. For example, if you started with a one-hundred-thousand-dollar life insurance program on your newborn child, it would be worth approximately twelve thousand dollars when the child reaches college age. This policy would cost you five hundred dollars per month. On the other hand, if you took the same five hundred dollars a month and put it into the appropriate mutual fund family, you would create a college fund of more than ninety thousand dollars over the same amount of time.

Never use insurance as an investment. The same is true for any insurance purchase, whether it is for your child's education, your retirement, or any other financial benefit. When you buy a life insurance policy, you should buy it solely for life insurance.

SAVE UP TO 80 PERCENT ON YOUR LIFE INSURANCE

To be able to save money on your life insurance, you must understand the three types of life insurance that are available:

1. whole life
2. universal life
3. term life

Whole Life Insurance

Whole life insurance has been responsible for leading thousands, if not millions, of individuals to invest in insurance policies instead of buying straight term insurance.

Whole life insurance is intended to be a method of investment in which you can build cash value at the same time as receiving insurance coverage. Basically, a certain amount of your monthly premium goes toward your insurance coverage and the rest goes toward investment. Cash value refers to the investment portion of the policy. This type of insurance sometimes has a 300 to 400 percent markup over term insurance. Whole life policies can be dressed up or down, depending on the information given by the salesperson and what the individual wants to achieve. Whole life policies usually have level premiums and claim to build tax-deferred cash value. "Tax-deferred cash value" is a nice-sounding term, but it has no value whatsoever to the insured. When you die, the cash value remains with the insurance company. The beneficiary receives only the policy's face value.

There are a number of marketing gimmicks that are used when whole life insurance is presented. Once you take a look at the major promises and examine the actual results, you see that in most cases, whole life insurance is not a sound purchase for the majority of individuals. Listed below are a few misleading claims concerning whole life insurance:

$ "You can borrow against your cash value." With whole life insurance, the insurance company tells you that, as your cash value grows, you can borrow against it at low interest rates. This sounds good, but actually the insurance company is charging you interest on your own money. Moreover, if you borrow against your life insurance policy and do not repay the loan, the amount will be deducted from your death benefit.

$ "You earn interest on your insurance policy." When you examine whole life insurance, you find that the interest rate is normally the lowest in the financial market—it is usually between 1 and 2 percent (sometimes as high as 3 percent, depending on the market rate). Still, this seems like a benefit; but is it? As I indicated earlier, the cash value remains with the insurance company if you should die. The interest that you receive goes toward the cash value, not to the beneficiary whom you intended it to go to. This is another reason why you should not use insurance as an investment. If you want to earn interest, it would be better for you to invest in a no-load stock or bond fund.

$ "You will eventually have a paid-up insurance policy." Salespeople will tell you that if you pay a certain amount of money into your policy, you will have a paid-up policy. This means you will no longer have to pay premiums to maintain your insurance policy. You will have insurance without premiums.

However, take a closer look at paid-up policies. To receive one, you have to pay your premium for several years. The extra money you put in to *overpay* for your insurance will be used by the insurance company at some point in time to pay your premiums. In essence, what you will have done is to put in enough money so that the interest will pay your premiums. You can have a much better return if you invest your own money.

$ "Your insurance is a tax shelter." The implication here is that life insurance has some type of special tax benefits. The salesperson will tell you that you can borrow money from your insurance policy tax free. Big deal! Anytime you borrow money from the bank or any other place, it is always tax free. Income tax is not charged on borrowed money; therefore, this is a completely invalid statement.

Insurance companies also claim that upon your death, your life insurance benefits are tax exempt. In fact, after a person dies, income tax is not charged on any part of that person's property. However, insurance benefits and the other parts of the estate are subject to estate taxes, under certain conditions. You are led to believe that the insurance company has something to do with tax benefits, but it does not.

$ "Buy insurance while you are young and save money." Insurance premiums are lower when you are younger, but the longer you pay into the insurance company, the more money the insurance company makes. Money can be a progressive asset if it is properly invested.

Remember that the purpose of insurance is to protect your financial assets for your family after you die. If you don't have any assets, you do not have a need for life insurance.

Universal Life Insurance

Universal life insurance is much like whole life in the sense that it has many hidden charges that keep the money with the insurance company. Universal life is basically a term life policy with some type of investment plan included. The investment aspect of the policy is flexible to the extent that you can use different types of investment vehicles. The investment part of the premium can be set up in a fixed-rate account or be self-directed into some type of mutual fund.

The way universal life insurance works is that the premium cost is set above the insurance cost. Once the premium and other charges have been paid, the balance of your money goes into the investment. Because of the high cost of insurance fees and commissions, only a portion of your money ever gets to the investment account.

Usually, you are told that you are getting a guaranteed rate on your money. In reality, you only get the guaranteed rate on the money that actually gets to the investment account.

For example, a person buys a universal life policy with a one-hundred-thousand-dollar death benefit and is promised a 10 percent return for twenty years. Suppose the premium is two thousand dollars per year. The insured is paid only on the money that goes into the investment account. Assume that the person starts the first year by paying the two-thousand-dollar premium up front. Fees and the cost of the insurance are deducted from this premium amount. It is possible that 30 percent of the two thousand dollars will be deducted just to open the account. In other words, instead of investing two thousand dollars, the insured has only fourteen hundred dollars left to go into the investment account.

In addition, this investment probably will earn less than 6 percent per year. Each year, the policy carries other hidden costs, and the cost of the term insurance also is going to go up each year, both further reducing the amount that goes into your investment account. Most people never recognize these extra charges and fees because their premium stays the same.

Watch out for the fine print. Universal life policies may state that they will pay you a guaranteed 10 percent, but if you take your money out of the policy, the amount of the proceeds can drop as much as 50 percent.

Action Step

Avoid buying low-interest
insurance policies.

Term Life

Term life insurance is the life insurance people should be buying instead of whole life or universal life. This is actual insurance and does not include investment plans or hidden charges. Moreover, term insurance is the least expensive of all life insurance. You can save up to 80 percent of the cost of whole life or universal life.

Action Step

Buy term life insurance, and save
the difference.

As I stated earlier, you should not combine insurance and investment in one package. If you have an insurance need, I suggest that you purchase term life and take the balance that you would be paying into a whole life policy and put it in a mutual fund.

There are three types of term insurance:

$ Annual renewal term: In this type of insurance, a policy is purchased for a period of one year. At the end of that year, you receive a statement so that you can renew the policy for another year. The insurance increases a few dollars each year, but the insurance is guaranteed to be renewable every year if you pay your premium. This is perhaps the best type of insurance for a growing family.

$ Decreasing term: This type allows you to pay premiums that remain the same, but the amount of the insurance decreases. Decreasing term is used primarily as mortgage insurance to cover homes and other items for which you will want to drop the insurance coverage after the product that is financed has been paid off.

$ Level premium term: This type allows you to choose a policy for five, ten, or fifteen years. Your premium and the amount of insurance remain the same. With level premium term, you will pay more for the premium in the early years, but the difference balances out over the term of the policy.

SUMMARIZING INSURANCE

As you can see, there are many types of insurance. They all have a purpose, and the cost varies from one insurance company to another. You should eliminate insurance waste whenever you can. Examine your policies to make sure that the coverage is right for you, and do not depend on the agent or insurance company to do this for you. Because there are so many factors involved and because insurance varies from state to state, it is wise to find a good financial advisor who can help you to obtain the best insurance for you and your family.

The chart at the end of this chapter lists the various types of insurance available. It will give you an idea of the kinds of savings you may be able to obtain by reducing your overall insurance costs. Use this information in conjunction with what has been presented in this chapter.

PRACTICAL APPLICATION

Review the above "Types of Insurance" chart (table 4) and compare your current insurance policies to it.

TABLE 4
Types of Insurance*

Type of Insurance	Before	After	Net Savings
Auto Insurance	$1,500	$ 800	+ $ 700
Whole Life Insurance	1,500	0	+ 1,500
Universal Life Insurance	0	0	0
Term Life Insurance	0	360	− 360
Debit Life Insurance	225	0	+ 225
Cancer & Other Specialty Policies	250	0	+ 250
Mortgage Insurance	700	375	+ 325
Hospitalization Insurance	1,500	1,000	+ 500
Disability	500	0	+ 500
Homeowners' Insurance	400	300	+ 100
Umbrella Insurance Policy	0	160	− 160

*This chart shows the kinds of savings that may be obtained by reducing overall insurance costs. The "Before" column represents what the policyholder is currently paying for insurance. The "After" column indicates what his or her insurance costs could be after implementing the recommendations in this chapter. The last column shows what the policyholder's net savings could be. These amounts are approximate and will vary from individual to individual.

CHAPTER 11

TRAINING YOUR CHILDREN TO MANAGE MONEY

*Train up a child in the way he should go: and when he is old, he
will not depart from it.*
—Proverbs 22:6

*Therefore shall ye lay up these my words in your heart and in
your soul, and bind them for a sign upon your hand, that they
may be as frontlets between your eyes. And ye shall teach them
your children, speaking of them when thou sittest in thine house,
and when thou walkest by the way, when thou liest down, and
when thou risest up. And thou shalt write them upon the door
posts of thine house, and upon thy gates: that your days may be
multiplied, and the days of your children, in the land which the
LORD sware unto your fathers to give them,
as the days of heaven upon the earth.*
—Deuteronomy 11:18–21

Richard told me a sad story of his grandfather, who once
had owned 2,800 acres of prime timberland in Alabama.
"My grandfather died at age fifty-five," he said. "He
lived most of his life as a logger. He had seven children, five
boys and two girls. One of the boys died early, which left six
children. My grandfather was considered a good businessman,
even though he lived in a small town.

"Over the years, working with his sons, he accumulated this
large tract of land. He bought the land, cut and sold the timber,

and paid for the land, one tract at a time. He continued until he owned twenty-eight hundred acres, and over the years his land appreciated in value because of a hunting camp he had opened on the Dog River."

As Richard continued, he explained why he thought it was important for a family to organize its financial affairs. "My grandfather's main possession was his property. When he died unexpectedly and without a will, my grandmother did not receive full ownership of the property. She received an equal share with the children.

"Grandmother loved all of her children and could not decide what was the best way to proceed. Every time the family talked about how to divide the land they had inherited in order to keep the property in the family, no plan ever materialized. One recommendation was to take the plots, divide them into seven parcels, and let each child draw a number. This did not work because they all feared they might draw the lowlands, and this would be unfair.

"Since they could not agree on any settlement, they were forced to sell the land. Grandmother was allowed to keep the homestead. The money was divided equally between my father and his brothers and sisters.

"This turned out to be one of the worst options but seemed the only way to settle the matter. Within five years, the two sisters used their shares to buy homes in Detroit. Two of the brothers bought property in other locations. The other two unwisely spent their share of the money and went completely broke."

As Richard concluded his story, I was taken with the harsh reality of it, but at the same time, I realized that many similar cases exist. "At every family meeting," Richard said, "there were arguments about the property. The equal shares scenario totally split the family apart. No one had controlling authority. The bad thing about this whole situation was that seven years later, they discovered oil on the tract next to Dog River."

From this example, we can see that Richard's grandfather had been a hard worker and a good provider, and he had wanted the best for his family. Even though he had been all of these things, he had never made provisions for his property or taught his children how to manage it. Consequently, his lifetime possessions were not directed in the way he had intended, which was to stay in the family for its benefit.

This story illustrates how crucial it is for families to do estate financial planning, and to learn what are the legal ramifications if one or both parents should die without a will and without making adequate financial provisions. The Scriptures say, *"A good man leaves an inheritance to his children's children"* (Proverbs 13:22 NKJV). To establish a strong financial legacy, you must first consult a reputable financial planner so that you can make the proper provisions regarding your estate. The next step is to help your children to learn and implement sound financial principles. The following information will help you to accomplish this.

ENSURE YOUR CHILDREN'S FINANCIAL FUTURE

It is our responsibility as parents to teach our children how to handle money. Most children do not start to learn how to handle money until after they leave home.

The best training for your children is for them to develop and implement good money management skills early in life. Children learn many personal skills in the early years of their lives from observing how their parents do things. Therefore, it is necessary for you, as a parent, to give your children a good model to emulate. To teach them how to manage money according to biblical guidelines, you must first learn how to apply the biblical principles in your own life.

Parents must realize that their attitudes and ways of spending money greatly influence children. By being good examples in the way they handle money, parents train their children to become good stewards over the resources with which they are entrusted.

BUDGETING

An allowance will give a child the opportunity to handle his or her own money. Usually, a child is ready to receive an allowance even before beginning school.

Through an allowance, a child is given a certain amount of money per week as his or her share of the family income. In turn, the child is assigned various chores to help with the family's work. If the work is not completed, the child does not receive any allowance.

The amount of the weekly allowance depends on the child's age, the needs of the child, and the financial circumstances of the family. The most important thing is not the amount of allowance that is given, but that a child learns to be responsible in handling money.

Parents may give advice and guidance on how to handle money, but a child has to have the freedom to decide how to spend the allowance. In the end, the child must learn to make the final decision. This will enable him or her to learn by trial and error. When a child finds that spending his or her whole allowance on a single item, such as a bag of popcorn, means that he or she will have to wait a whole week before buying something else, the youngster starts to watch spending more closely. The child begins to examine the need to buy or to save. As the child grows, his or her capability of handling money also matures, and the amount of the allowance may be gradually increased.

THE THREE-JAR METHOD

When teaching a child to budget, begin by enabling the child to learn firsthand the impact of living off of 70 percent of his or her income. I believe the best way to do this is by the "Three-Jar Method." Set up three jars labeled by category—10 percent giving (tithes), 10 percent short-term savings, and 10 percent long-term savings. From the very beginning, the remaining 70 percent is the money the child may use to spend on whatever he or she wants to purchase. This teaches the child to save and pay cash for what he or she wants to buy. Each week as the allowance is given, the child deposits money into each jar. Even a young child can understand this procedure. He or she learns that there is no more money to spend when the remaining 70 percent is gone. When training a child to budget, the objective should be to gradually increase responsibility until the child is independent in managing money.

From the time our children were six years old, they understood the Three-Jar Method. The way my ten-year-old daughter handled her allowance was to give 10 percent to the church, place 20 percent in her bank savings account, and save 70 percent in a special place. Many times she ended up with almost 90 percent of her money in savings. As she grew older, she began to realize the advantage of saving to have money to spend when everyone else was out of money. She comprehended the concept of delayed gratification.

My son took his tithe to church, and although he stuffed his long-term savings and short-term savings in the same jar, he still maintained the concept. The problem, however, was that he would spend every dime he got his hands on over the 30 percent. My son, like many other young people, began to develop an appetite for brand name tennis shoes and designer jeans. Although he was being faithful in setting aside the 30 percent, he did not seem to be developing in some of the other financial areas.

One day I discussed this point with my wife. I said, "If we allow him the opportunity to purchase his own tennis shoes and clothes, then he will make better choices about spending." We decided that the incentive would be to let him keep the money he saved.

We noticed that this began to have an immediate impact. He began to be more responsible in his spending habits. He began to buy less expensive items and keep the difference. Therefore, we decided to let him have his own checking account to pay for such things as clothes, school supplies, and tuition. We assisted him in setting up the right account with no monthly fees or service charges. We explained that if he maintained the account properly (no bounced checks), he would receive a significant increase in his allowance. I showed him how to balance his account each month and explained the cost of a bounced check.

Our son has become aware of every dime that goes through his checking account. He balances his checkbook each month and knows how much money he has available to spend. This maturity came as a result of our increasing his responsibilities and income when he was faithful with smaller amounts.

ESTABLISHING AN ATTITUDE OF GIVING

The best way to establish an attitude of giving in your child is to encourage it when the child is young. This works best when children are allowed to give and can tangibly see that their giving is beneficial. A child will better understand the impact of giving when he or she contributes in ways such as helping to support orphans, buying food for the needy and homeless, or giving to missions.

It is also good for children to participate in a family prayer time each week for worship and for dedicating the week's gifts to the Lord.

SHOULD YOU GIVE CHILDREN OFFERING MONEY?

In my opinion, giving is part of our worship of God. When I was growing up, I used to sit next to my mother in church, wiggling like any other five-year-old. But when the offering plate came by, my mother would take a coin and let me drop it into the plate. After the plate went by, I was back to my own regular activities, not realizing that there was any special significance to the offering.

Instead of allowing a child to drop a coin into the offering plate, I believe the best way to train children to be faithful is to give them something with which to be faithful. Give them an allowance and teach them why they should make a contribution to the offering. Teach them to use 10 percent of their money as an offering as part of their worship of God. Lead them to understand that they are giving this out of obedience and love for Him.

This teaching should be based on the biblical principle we learned in chapter 3, "Planning and Preparation." All that we have belongs to God, and while we are here on earth, He is allowing us to take care of it, to be stewards of it. Therefore, we are to use it wisely.

CHAPTER 12

FAITH FOR GOD'S SUPERNATURAL INCREASE

*Whosoever shall say unto this mountain, Be thou removed, and
be thou cast into the sea; and shall not doubt in his heart, but
shall believe that those things which he saith shall come to pass;
he shall have whatsoever he saith. Therefore I say unto you,
What things soever ye desire, when ye pray, believe that ye receive
them, and ye shall have them.*
—Mark 11:23–24

*And God is able to make all grace abound toward you; that ye,
always having all sufficiency in all things, may abound
to every good work.*
—2 Corinthians 9:8

Faith can change financial circumstances. The first step of faith is to believe you can do what God says you can do and that you can have what God says you can have.

God operates a fail-safe financial system that is stacked in favor of the believer. However, you first must learn how to get the most out of what you have. You must be a good steward and manage what you have already been given. This step is completely separate and is absolutely necessary. It must be mastered before you can walk fully in God's supernatural provisions. After you have learned how to properly manage what you have, then you are ready to use your faith and to expect to receive an increase in your resources. Even if you have made every financial mistake possible, if you repent and start to operate under God's financial plan, God will honor your faith.

If you are in a situation in which you don't have enough money coming in to meet your financial needs, or you are caught in circumstances in which you are locked into the poverty cycle, you must first learn to be faithful with the money and resources you have. God can change financial circumstances, but you must take a step of faith (some action) in order for something to come your way other than what you currently have. It will more than likely require extra effort on your part, but remember that the victory will only come to those who are willing to work to overcome their situations.

RECEIVING GOD'S SUPERNATURAL INCREASE

The life of Joseph is an excellent example of good stewardship and what it means to trust God to supply one's needs. Joseph had been sold into slavery, but God blessed him in spite of his economic circumstances. The Bible states that Joseph was a successful man, and that God blessed Joseph's master, Potiphar, for Joseph's sake:

> And Joseph was brought down to Egypt; and Potiphar, an officer of Pharaoh, captain of the guard, an Egyptian, bought him of the hands of the Ishmeelites, which had brought him down thither. And the LORD was with Joseph, and he was a prosperous man; and he was in the house of his master the Egyptian. And his master saw that the LORD was with him, and that the LORD made all that he did to prosper in his hand. (Genesis 39:1–3)

Joseph had nothing when he was taken to Egypt, not even the coat of many colors that had been given to him by his father (Genesis 37:3). But, by being faithful with what he had been given and faithful to God's Word, he was able to change the economic destiny of an entire nation and walk in the supernatural provision God had destined for his life.

And Pharaoh said unto Joseph, See, I have set thee over all the land of Egypt. And Pharaoh took off his ring from his hand, and put it upon Joseph's hand, and arrayed him in vestures of fine linen, and put a gold chain about his neck; and he made him to ride in the second chariot which he had; and they cried before him, Bow the knee: and he made him ruler over all the land of Egypt. And Pharaoh said unto Joseph, I am Pharaoh, and without thee shall no man lift up his hand or foot in all the land of Egypt.

(Genesis 41:41–44)

What was it about Joseph that made him so successful in spite of his difficult circumstances? What was it that Potiphar saw? What were the principles that Joseph used that were so powerful they could change the economic destiny of an entire nation? What was it that Joseph did that caused God to act on his behalf? What economic principles and biblical guidelines do we need to glean from these Scriptures in order to gain an understanding that will affect our economic heritage?

LOOKING PAST POVERTY TO PROSPERITY

God wants us to be prepared in order to receive supernatural increase. According to the Bible, world conditions will get worse and worse; but as the world deteriorates, God will bless the church both spiritually and financially. He will raise up individuals within the local church who have proven to be faithful and trustworthy stewards. He will give them the wealth of the world in order to finance the end-time harvest.

The wealth of the sinner is laid up for the just.

(Proverbs 13:22)

Ye rich men, weep and howl for your miseries that shall come upon you. Your riches are corrupted, and your garments are motheaten. Your gold and silver is cankered....Ye have heaped treasure together for the last days.

(James 5:1–3)

Just as in Joseph's day, many people today are slaves to the world's economic system, held captive by myths, religious traditions, and wrong attitudes about handling money. Many have made debt their master and overseer. They are in bondage to their jobs or the money their jobs provide. They bow down and make a monthly pilgrimage to the god of instant gratification (the credit card), often paying more in interest to the world's economic system than they give to God. Even if they wanted to do something for the kingdom of God, they wouldn't be able to because they are barely able to take care of themselves. They are locked in prison without ever realizing that there is a way out.

God wants us to prosper spiritually, mentally, physically, and financially. God wants us to break the bondage in our lives so that we can become true stewards for Him. He wants us to become free so that we can have an impact for the kingdom of God.

God desires to raise up stewards whom He can trust to use their faith to receive supernatural increase. The increase is not merely to meet their needs, but also to help meet the needs of others and to establish God's covenant in the earth for the end-time harvest of souls. *"But thou shalt remember the LORD thy God: for it is he that giveth thee power to get wealth, that he may establish his covenant"* (Deuteronomy 8:18).

God has put within every individual the desire to do great things—the desire to help one's fellowman, one's race, one's community, and one's nation. God has given all of us gifts, creative talents, and ideas that could immediately change the financial circumstances of our lives. However, most people live unfulfilled lives. They think, "If only we had the money to develop our ideas." Yet, while Joseph was in prison with no money, he flourished like a flower.

Action Step

Use the gifts and talents God has
already given you.

Most people suppress the gifts that God has instilled in them and give up on their creative ideas because of their circumstances. They use excuses like, "I have no money," "I have no credit," "I was born on the wrong side of the tracks," or any number of other obstacles that are seemingly beyond their control, to keep them from fulfilling the creative desires God has instilled in them. Therefore, desires die on the vine and never come to fruition! They never fulfill their purpose in life. They never walk in their inheritance.

In this chapter, we will take a close look at how to develop the creative ideas that God has given us. In chapters 1–5, we looked at the fundamental principles outlined in the Bible that show how to build a foundation to handle God's wealth and what to do with the resources once they have been entrusted to our care. Now, we will look at what it means to have faith for God's supernatural increase. If you have already demonstrated your faithfulness in properly managing what you have, you can expect immediate results.

I have placed this section last for a reason. If a person receives wealth without knowing how to handle it, it will disappear. The Bible points this out through the Scriptures: *"Wilt thou set thine eyes upon that which is not? for riches certainly make themselves wings; they fly away as an eagle toward heaven"* (Proverbs 23:5).

FAITH IS BEING PREPARED TO RECEIVE

God has reminded me about some things concerning fishing. First of all, He has reminded me that to catch a fish, you must have your line in the water. To catch a larger fish, you might even have to move to a larger pond (where the big fish are). You might have to launch farther out into the deep water. You might have to prepare for a larger increase. You might have to get a larger boat and heavier equipment.

However, most of all, you must be prepared to handle the big fish when you get him in the boat, or the fish could either sink your small boat or swallow you up. Joseph was prepared when his time came because he never stopped using the talents and gifts God had given him. He kept his faith line in the water.

Unless you cast your line into the water, you will not catch a fish. A person who wants to plug into God's supernatural blessings must prepare himself or herself to receive the blessings before they come. A proper foundation must be laid. We must know the biblical principles that govern money.

Action Step

Prepare to receive your blessing
before it comes.

DEVELOPING YOUR CREATIVE IDEAS

The gospel of Luke gives us some important biblical guidelines for governing money. Luke 16:9 says, *"And I say unto you, Make to yourselves friends of the mammon of unrighteousness; that, when ye fail, they may receive you into everlasting habitations"* (Luke 16:9), which may also be translated, *"I tell you, use worldly wealth to gain friends for yourselves, so that when it is gone, you will be welcomed into eternal dwellings"* (NIV). In addition, Luke 16:12 asks a probing question about stewardship: *"And if ye have not been faithful in that which is another man's, who shall give you that which is your own?"* In other words, if you are not faithful with another man's property, who will give you your own property?

Review chapters 1–6, which deal with the stewardship principle, planning and preparation, debt, honesty and integrity, and giving. If you have been a faithful and wise steward of the resources you have been given, and if you have been applying biblical principles of stewardship, you should already see the evidence of God's increase in your life. You have become experienced by being a good manager of other people's property first.

Once you have used other people's property faithfully and well, you can develop your own creative ideas. First, prepare a written plan of action. Research the cost and income figures. How much will it take to produce the service or finished product? How much do you need to advertise and market it?

Make sure your ideas are clear to you and that you can explain them clearly to others. There are opportunities all around you. It doesn't matter if the economy is going down or up; there is always room for creative ideas. However, most opportunities are going to require action on your part. They may require that you change some old habits. You may have to get a second job, or even go back to school.

Action Step

After God gives you an idea, be willing to change your lifestyle.

Keep your faith line in the water. While you are developing a written plan, don't let Satan steal your idea or your desire to fulfill it. Don't be discouraged by those who don't understand. Stay away from those who will dash cold water on your desires. Be willing to change your lifestyle.

Action Step

Start from where you are, and be faithful with what you have.

Don't develop any new bills or try to borrow money until you have tested your idea. Make sure there is a market for it. Use the money you have in your savings or the creative gift that God has already put inside you to develop the idea and a plan of action that is self-financing. If you have a good idea, it does not always take money.

Action Step

Ask God to show you how to develop your creative ideas.

I remember the first business I started. I only had the idea and the energy; someone else put up the money. I worked and provided the manpower, and we split the profit.

In the second business I started, God gave me an idea to market a new product. I developed the marketing concept and borrowed money to buy the first unit. I let the lender keep the product as collateral. When we sold the product, there was enough profit to pay the lender and buy new items for inventory, which I owned 100 percent.

THE EXAMPLE OF JOSEPH

As I wrote earlier, there are economic principles and biblical guidelines that we can glean from the life of Joseph that will provide us with an understanding that will affect our economic heritage. There are several things that stand out about Joseph:

1. He never forgot the promise that God had given him. He could see where he was headed based on God's promise (Genesis 37:6–9), not on the circumstances that held him captive.

2. Joseph made the most out of what he had. He played the hand he had been dealt. He acted on what God had given to him, no matter what his circumstances were. He worked as if he were working for the Lord; he was obedient to God's holy calling.

3. He never forgot that he was a servant of the almighty God, even though he was in prison and in bondage to another man.

4. He used the talents he had for the benefit of the person he was serving as a slave, but he always gave glory to God for these talents.

5. He was a giver. He gave out of what he had. He never forsook his gifts simply because he did not have money or freedom, or when he was misused or treated unfairly. He blossomed where he was.

6. He shared his gifts with everyone he encountered, whether the person had money or not.

Because of his faithfulness with what he had been entrusted, Joseph was a man who could be trusted by God and man!

God knows the condition of our hearts. He cannot operate to His fullest capacity in those who are not faithful with the finances He has already entrusted to their care. As stewards, we must learn to follow the instruction that God has given us and not waste God's money. We must learn the true purpose of wealth in the lives of Christians and be willing to be coworkers with God to establish His covenant in the earth.

Yes, God still answers prayer, but He can only give true wealth to those who have prepared themselves in advance and know how to handle it. We must use our faith to develop the resources if we do not have money or wealth. It takes obedience to walk in the inheritance that God has set in place for us from the foundation of the world.

Remember that as God's stewards, the resources with which He has entrusted us belong to Him. They will be in our trust (care) only for a short period of time while we are on earth. This does not mean that God does not want us to enjoy their benefits while we live here, but He does not want us to consume them all on ourselves. He wants us to help Him establish His covenant on earth. Again, we should remember the principle God clearly outlines in Deuteronomy 8:18: *"But thou shalt remember the LORD thy God: for it is he that giveth thee power to get wealth, that he may establish his covenant which he sware unto thy fathers"* (Deuteronomy 8:18).

Jesus made this principle even clearer in His discussion with Peter, recorded in the tenth chapter of Mark:

> *"I tell you the truth," Jesus replied, "no one who has left home [possessions] or brothers or sisters or mother or father or children or fields [possessions] for me and the gospel will fail to receive a hundred times as much in this present age (homes, brothers, sisters, mothers, children and fields—and with them, persecutions) and in the age to come, eternal life.*   (Mark 10:29–30 NIV)

Jesus said we would receive *"a hundred times as much in this present age,"* but the condition is that we live for Jesus' sake and for the Gospel.

As stewards, we must remember that all worldly wealth and material possessions will remain on the earth. It is what we do with what has been entrusted to us here on earth that has an impact for Jesus and the kingdom of God. It is only what we have done with what we have received that will benefit us when we get to heaven: How many souls did we impact for God? What did we do for the poor? Did we get the maximum benefit from what we had? Did we use our faith to do what we were instructed to do? Did we fulfill our purpose in life?

ACT ON YOUR ECONOMIC DESTINY

Now, you must act on what you have learned! I have covered principles that have changed the lives and destinies of countless thousands. Yet, knowledge alone will not get the job done. Now that you know that God has a financial system, you must be able to apply His economic principles to your life. You must act on what you have learned.

Action Step

Act on God's financial plan in order to change your financial circumstances.

Do you remember the example from 1 Kings 17:8–16? The widow of Zarephath was down to a cake and a handful of meal when the prophet Elijah came to her. She had nothing left. However, because of her obedience and faithfulness to do what the word of God said through Elijah, her needs were met and she did not lack anything.

If the widow had not obeyed the word of the Lord, she would not have received the blessing God had for her. She and her son would have died of starvation. Yet, because of her obedience in acting on the word of God, God changed her whole situation from that of death to life!

Ask God in faith to show you what to do or how to use what you already have. Ask Him to give you a creative idea. God can change your circumstances, but you must be willing to act. You must put your faith line in the water and expect to land a financial blessing.

Action Step

Remember that faith without
action is dead.

STARTING A BUSINESS TO GENERATE ADDITIONAL INCOME

Ask God for a good business idea. One of the best ways to generate income is to identify something you would enjoy doing and use it to provide a service for others. This could be your hobby, or the hobby of someone you know.

If you currently have a job working for someone else, examine the possibility of marketing the same service on an independent basis. The main idea is to identify a market to which you could supply a product or service.

A good place to start is to examine existing businesses that have been successful in your area of interest. The possibilities are unlimited. Ask the Lord to give you an understanding of how to make your service or product valuable to other people. It is a good idea to do research at the library; you will find many books and articles on how to start and develop a new business.

GET WISE COUNSEL

Call the Small Business Administration (SBA) office in your city and ask for information and assistance. The SBA's Service Core of Retired Executives (SCORE) conducts seminars on various aspects of starting and building a small business. Another way to get good advice is to contact Christians who have businesses and experience in your area of interest.

How to Activate Your Faith

To receive God's supernatural increase, you must be faithful and you must apply faith to your financial circumstances. First, you must exercise your faith to believe it is possible for you to walk in the provisions outlined in the Scriptures. Secondly, you must exercise faith to take the action steps necessary to apply the biblical principles to your financial circumstances.

To activate your faith, you must identify the scriptural promises that relate to your particular condition or circumstances. Then, you must stand on these Scriptures. Make them a part of you and a part of your daily devotions.

Listed below are personalized Scriptures that relate to financial increase. You should meditate on these Scriptures daily. Put them on index cards and speak them out loud in the morning and before you go to bed at night.

Use the Scriptures listed below in conjunction with the twenty-one practical steps to building wealth in God's economy found in chapter 13. As you apply these action steps to your circumstances, you will see the power of God start to work in your life to change your financial situation.

Personalized Scriptures for Financial Increase

This book of the law will not depart out of my mouth, but I will meditate on it day and night, that I may observe to do according to all that is written in it. For then God will make my way prosperous, and then I will have good success (Joshua 1:8).

I seek first the kingdom of God and His righteousness, so all these things will be added to me (Matthew 6:33).

I will remember the Lord my God, for it is He who gives me power to get wealth so that He may establish His covenant that He swore to my forefathers (Deuteronomy 8:18).

The Lord desires above all things that I may prosper and be in health, even as my soul prospers (3 John 2).

The Lord has pleasure in my prosperity, since I am His servant (Psalm 35:27).

My God will supply all my needs according to His riches in glory by Christ Jesus (Philippians 4:19).

The Lord will open to me His good treasure—the heavens to give rain to my land in His season, and to bless all the work of my hands; and I will lend to many nations, and I will not borrow. The Lord will make me the head, and not the tail; and I will be above only, and I will not be beneath if I listen to the commandments of the Lord my God, to observe and to do them (Deuteronomy 28:12–13).

The Lord my God teaches me to profit, and leads me in the way that I should go (Isaiah 48:17).

I seek the Lord, so I will not lack any good thing (Psalm 34:10).

He who did not spare His own Son, but delivered Him up for us all, will also freely give me all things (Romans 8:32).

Christ has redeemed me from the curse of the law, being made a curse for me so that the blessing of Abraham might come on me (Galatians 3:13–14).

God will go before me and make the crooked places straight. He will break the gates of brass in pieces, and cut the bars of iron in two. And He will give me the treasures of darkness, and hidden riches of secret places (Isaiah 45:2–3).

I am willing and obedient, so I will eat the good of the land (Isaiah 1:19).

I obey and serve God, so I will spend my days in prosperity, and my years in pleasures (Job 36:11).

I know the grace of my Lord Jesus Christ, that He was rich, yet for my sake He became poor so that I, through His poverty, might be rich (2 Corinthians 8:9).

The wealth of the sinner is laid up for me, the righteous (Proverbs 13:22).

I am faithful, so I will abound with blessings (Proverbs 28:20).

I delight in the Lord, and He will give me the desires of my heart (Psalm 37:4).

God is doing exceedingly abundantly above all that I ask or think, according to the power that works in me (Ephesians 3:20).

God has given to me all things that pertain to life and godliness, through the knowledge of Him who has called me to glory and virtue (2 Peter 1:3).

I give, and it will be given to me. Good measure, pressed down, shaken together, and running over, will men give to me (Luke 6:38).

I am not slothful, but I am a follower of those who through faith and patience inherit the promises (Hebrews 6:12).

Jesus came that I might have life, and that I might have it more abundantly (John 10:10).

Jesus is my mediator of a better covenant, which was established upon better promises (Hebrews 8:6).

I do not fear, for it is my Father's good pleasure to give me the kingdom (Luke 12:32).

The blessings of the Lord make me rich, and He adds no sorrow to them (Proverbs 10:22).

I do not grow weary in doing good; therefore, in due season I will reap, if I do not give up (Galatians 6:9).

PRACTICAL APPLICATION

One of the biggest problems I have had as a businessman since I asked God for creative ideas has been a proper balance of time. After God gives you an idea for a business to break the economic bondage in your life, the Devil tries to use the business to take away your time with God.

I have listed below several points you should remember as God starts giving you creative ideas:

$ Give God the credit and glory! Keep your priorities straight. Ask the Lord to guide you in doing this.
$ Give God your time.
$ Trust in God's provision. Let Him be responsible for bringing in the money to make the business succeed.
$ Be patient and content; cast your care on the Lord. Don't try to carry the load yourself.

CHAPTER 13

TWENTY-ONE STEPS TO BUILDING WEALTH

Even so faith, if it hath not works [corresponding actions], is dead, being alone. Yea, a man may say, Thou hast faith, and I have works: show me thy faith without thy works, and I will show thee my faith by my works.
—James 2:17–18

Be thou diligent to know the state of thy flocks [business affairs], and look well to thy herds. For riches are not for ever: and doth the crown endure to every generation?
—Proverbs 27:23–24

Having financial surplus is a natural by-product of operating in God's financial system. It doesn't matter what your race or economic background is. As a steward, God expects you to use the ability that He has given you to manage and build resources. It doesn't matter where you start; it is where you end that counts. The starting point might be different for each individual, but God expects you to be a doer of the Word. He expects you to get started and be faithful in the process.

As I wrote in the last chapter, in order to build wealth in God's economy, you must believe that it is possible for you to do what God says you can do and that you can have the financial resources that God says you can have. Then you must take action! The secret to learning how to operate in God's financial system is to realize that you must do your part in order for God to do His part. There are basic steps that should be taken by every individual who is interested in building a sound financial foundation and operating within the guidelines of God's financial system.

The following twenty-one basic strategies incorporate the fundamental financial principles that are outlined in the Bible. They also summarize and integrate all the action steps that are included throughout this book. Every good financial plan will incorporate most, if not all, of these basic strategies. Use them as a checklist in organizing your financial plan.

STEP 1
Write Out Your Financial Goals

You must plan ahead to build wealth in God's financial system. First, tabulate your current financial condition to determine where you are—how much you own versus how much you owe. Secondly, from this financial statement, you should write out your financial goals: where you would like to be in the future (five, ten, even twenty years from now) in terms of your net worth, your income goals, your giving goals, your goals for saving, and your goals for education (for you and for your children). You must also make a realistic estimate of living expenses. Thirdly, you should write out your retirement goals. You must determine how much money you will need to have invested to live comfortably off the interest. These goals are important to your long-range success. Keep them in a safe place and refine them annually in your family's yearly planning meeting. Remember that it is never too soon to start planning, and that it is wise to consult a good financial planner to help you to achieve your financial goals wisely and effectively.

STEP 2
Live within Your Means

Control your spending by establishing a written budget. You can use your personal checking account to accomplish this purpose. Set up a payroll deduction plan with a goal of living on 70 percent of your income. Have 30 percent taken off the top before accounting for any living expenses. Never spend more than you earn. Remember, if you spend less than you earn, you will always have a surplus. This is a bedrock decision that must be made on your part. This is where you must draw your line in the sand. No matter what you earn, you must establish this as a minimum goal. When organizing your financial plan, remember that earning more is not the issue at this point! No matter how little or how much you earn, you must learn to live on less than you have coming in. Getting an increase is simple after you understand living within your means. If you are not willing to settle the issue of spending less than you earn, the other steps in this plan won't have any significant impact in changing your financial circumstances.

STEP 3
Set Aside Something from Every Paycheck

To start a wealth-building program, it is necessary to establish a surplus account. Building a surplus is essential to breaking the spirit of poverty and building long-term security. You should set aside a portion of every dollar you receive. After God, you should pay yourself first! Here is a good rule of thumb to establish in this regard: Whenever you write out a check to your church, you should be able to set aside (at a minimum) an equal amount for your savings. This establishes your surplus account. If you cannot start with 10 percent, take a step of faith to start setting aside something. This is another bedrock decision of your financial plan. If you don't make a firm commitment to this, you will always be at the mercy of your financial circumstances. Make a quality decision to start, and don't back out of it. Drive your stake in the ground. Set aside something, even if you only set aside one dollar a week until you can see better times.

STEP 4
Set Up a Short-Term Contingency Account

When you start your savings program, the first money should go toward your contingency account. This account should have enough money to cover three to six months' living expenses. Convert the surplus funds from this account to a longer-term savings account as your funds accumulate. This account can also be used for short-term cash purchases to avoid long-term debt and interest payments. The contingency account is also used for giving above and beyond the tithe. This account will give you financial stability and enable you to provide for your needs and to prosper, despite unexpected circumstances.

STEP 5
Keep Proper Records

Using your checking account is the easiest way to accomplish this. To move toward your financial goals, you must have an accurate picture of where you are to determine if you are on target. Open a free checking account with no monthly fee or service charges. Run all of your income through your checking account so that you will have a clear record of your income and expenditures. To form an accurate budget picture, it is very important to maintain this record.

STEP 6
Get Out of Debt

Understand the danger of surety and break the stronghold of debt in your life. The best way to avoid the debt trap is never to allow yourself to give in to temptation. If you are already overextended, establish a debt-reduction plan, with a goal to live debt free within three to five years, or with a maximum of 10 percent debt. Never purchase anything on your credit card unless you have the resources to pay off your purchases in full at the end of every month. The only way to break the habit is to stop all credit purchases until you get free of debt (especially credit card debt). Then, avoid putting yourself in a surety position ever again. Since principal and interest payments are the largest expense item for the average family, by eliminating these payments, many families will automatically increase their disposable incomes by as much as one-third. The savings can be applied to their surplus accounts.

STEP 7
Learn How to Make Money Work for You

Become familiar with how money works. It is important that you know the basic principles of investing and how compound interest works. Once you gain surplus funds, you must have a place to put them. You should learn how to get the best return possible on your savings with the minimum amount of risk. If you do not have the time to do this, you should get a good financial planner who will assist you in staying on track. It is essential for you to know what it feels like to have money (surplus) in your savings account. It is also important that you keep your financial goals in sight. Your overall investment strategy should be consistent with your written financial goals.

STEP 8
Open a No-Load or Rear-Load Mutual Fund

Pay no commission or low commission when establishing your long-term investment accounts. As your funds accumulate, you can move them from your short-term emergency account to your long-term investment accounts. For diversification purposes, most families will have a number of mutual fund accounts—money market fund, bond fund, and stock fund (or a combination of these funds).

STEP 9
Establish an IRA

Use a good family of mutual funds to open your individual retirement account (IRA). This will help you to earn the highest return on your long-term investment account. If you have a 401(k) or another company-sponsored retirement plan, you should set a goal of taking the maximum deduction allowed for matching retirement accounts. Some employers match one-to-one, others match two-to-one, and some even match three-to-one for every dollar the employee puts into the account. There are very few investments that can produce a greater return than a well-organized employer/employee retirement account.

STEP 10
Use Money Market Accounts

Let your money earn interest while it is in your checking account for your short-term emergency funds (or use an interest-bearing savings account with check-writing privileges). The interest rate on these accounts may vary depending on market circumstances. However, having a money market account always gives you immediate check-writing access to your short-term savings. In addition, you get interest income that would normally be lost.

STEP 11
Eliminate All Unnecessary Waste from Current Income

Get the maximum benefit from every dollar entrusted to your care. You dictate where your money goes, not the circumstances. Your goal is to manage every dime. Avoid every situation that robs you of your money (e.g., penalties, interest, fines, fees, tickets, late payments, fast-talking salespeople). Always be on the lookout for ways to reduce expenses and cut costs from your monthly budget.

STEP 12
Avoid Buying Insurance You May Not Need

You can save up to 80 percent on your life insurance if you buy term life insurance instead of whole life or universal life insurance. Invest the money you will save in your mutual fund or IRA account. You can also increase your wealth-building account by saving 40 to 50 percent on your automobile insurance. Increase the deductible from fifty dollars to a minimum of five hundred dollars on collision/comprehensive/liability insurance. Use your short-term emergency account to self-insure up to the five-hundred-dollar minimum.

Avoid purchasing credit life insurance, credit disability insurance, and extended warranties on credit purchases. Use your best judgment in this area. However, these are usually very expensive insurance policies that are always calculated heavily in favor of the insurance provider. Outside of principal and interest payments, insurance is one of the highest expense categories for the average family's budget. By eliminating unnecessary coverage on your life, auto, home, and miscellaneous insurance, many families can increase their disposable income by as much as 30 percent.

STEP 13
Reduce or Eliminate All Existing Interest Payments

Every dollar you spend on interest payments is money taken directly from your disposable income. It is gone forever! Every dollar you spend on interest is a dollar that could be working for you if it were placed in your interest-bearing investment account.

Your goal is to live debt free or to have a maximum of 10 percent debt. If you have credit cards that charge an 18 to 20 percent interest rate, save 10 percent on your credit card debt by refinancing your cards with a lower interest rate. Pay all credit card debts at the end of the month in which the purchase is made to avoid interest payments altogether (see step 6).

STEP 14
Save Up to 50 Percent on the Cost of an Automobile

When purchasing an automobile, you can save up to 50 percent if you buy a two-year-old automobile with low mileage and the same body style as the later models. Use this same principle when buying furniture. If you are just getting started as a young family, your main goal is to avoid debt (short- and long-term). Use the newspaper classified advertisements to find a good buy. (Don't be in a hurry.) Then pay cash!

STEP 15
Save 25 to 45 Percent on Home Purchases

If you buy your house wholesale at courthouse auctions, Veterans Administration (VA) or Federal Housing Administration (FHA) repossessions, or directly from bank repossession inventories, your savings can be between 25 and 45 percent.

STEP 16
Save over 30 Percent on Existing Home Mortgages

Refinance your house from a thirty-year mortgage to a fifteen-year mortgage at a lower interest rate. Depending on the interest rates at the time, you can cut your total interest payment by as much as one-third. You can also save substantial interest payments on your existing thirty-year mortgage by setting up a biweekly payment plan. If you pay your mortgage every two weeks instead of once a month, you will eliminate ten years of interest payments. For example, pay four hundred dollars every two weeks instead of eight hundred dollars each month. You can accomplish the same thing (and get the ten-year reduction) by making one extra monthly payment each year. (Make sure the extra payment goes directly to your principal. For more details, contact your financial planner.)

STEP 17
Learn How to Reduce Your Taxes

You should become familiar with the tax system. The average family spends 35 to 45 percent of its income on state and federal taxes (not including sales taxes). Most individuals can still make tax-deductible IRA contributions. Whenever possible, make the maximum contribution to your company retirement plan. There are also many expenses that are legitimate deductions when a person owns a small business. In addition, you can invest in tax-free mutual funds. There are legitimate ways to reduce your tax expenses to receive substantial savings. Ask your financial planner for additional help in this area.

STEP 18
Establish a Workable Estate Plan for Your Family

Prepare a will to avoid unnecessary court and probate costs. By establishing a workable estate plan, you can save on taxes and provide additional resources for your family.

STEP 19
Look for Creative Ways to Increase Current Income

After you realize that, as a good steward, you must live within your means, the next step is to use your faith to generate additional revenue. If you are not happy with your current income, it's time for a change in your lifestyle. Pray that God will give you creative ideas to utilize your existing talents. Ask God to reveal ways in which you can make yourself valuable to someone else. Identify a need in someone else's life and become a solution to that person's problem. Pray that the Lord will show you ways in which you can use what you have to produce more income. Ask Him for specific things that you can do, starting from where you are. Review chapter 11, "Faith for God's Supernatural Increase." Just one creative idea from God can significantly change your financial condition.

STEP 20
Plant a Seed to Help Others

Give of yourself in both time and money. After you begin to get your finances in order, look for an opportunity to help someone else. (Set aside a portion of your short-term savings specifically for this purpose.) You must be willing to share God's economic principles with others who need a financial breakthrough in their lives (your family, friends, and business acquaintances).

STEP 21
Be Patient

The greatest hindrance that prevents the average individual from walking in God's financial system is a lack of patience. Now that you know what God's financial plan is, you must be willing to act on it. But, financial freedom will not happen overnight. It could take three to five years for the average family that has serious financial problems to get out of debt and turn its finances around. The greatest temptation will be to try to rush this process. Set your course, establish your plan, and stick to it. The basics cannot be rushed. However, the time frame can be drastically reduced by adding faith to the equation. Give God an opportunity to work on your behalf.

GETTING YOUR FINANCES IN ORDER

For the average person, applying these twenty-one steps will require a major change in lifestyle. Remember that you do not have to do these steps in your own strength. If you will do your part, you will bring God on the scene, and He will do His part.

Ask God to give you the wisdom and understanding to be able to implement these twenty-one steps as He makes them real to you. In addition to putting into practice these action steps, go back to chapter 11, review the Scriptures on financial increase, and draw strength from them.

My prayer for you is that God will give you a revelation of the abundance that is available in His economic system, and that as you get your own finances in order, you will reach out to others and have an impact for the kingdom of God.

PRACTICAL APPLICATION

Use the "Twenty-One Steps to Building Wealth" in God's economy to organize your financial plan. For more information, contact Urban Impact Ministries. (The address and phone number may be found on the copyright page of this book.)

THE COMMITMENT

If you are serious about getting your financial house in order, you should fill in and sign the commitment form below. Make two copies; keep one in a prominent place, and send one to Urban Impact Ministries. (The address may be found on the copyright page of this book.)

To get my financial house in order, I realize I must do my part in order for God to do His part. I hereby make the following commitments:

1) I commit to changing the attitude and lifestyle that keep me in financial bondage, and I dedicate myself to becoming a good steward over what God has already entrusted to my care.
2) I commit to using my faith to break the spirit of poverty, to get out of debt (surety), and to expect God to bring financial increase in my life.
3) I commit to establishing a surplus account by spending less than I earn and setting aside something from each paycheck.
4) I commit to implementing the "Twenty-One Steps" plan outlined in chapter 12 and to opening a long-term savings account or an individual retirement account (IRA) this year by _____ (date).
5) I further commit to helping at least two other families get their finances in order by sharing the principles of financial increase.

Signature:_____

Please print:

Name _____

Address _____